THE PEAK DISTRICT

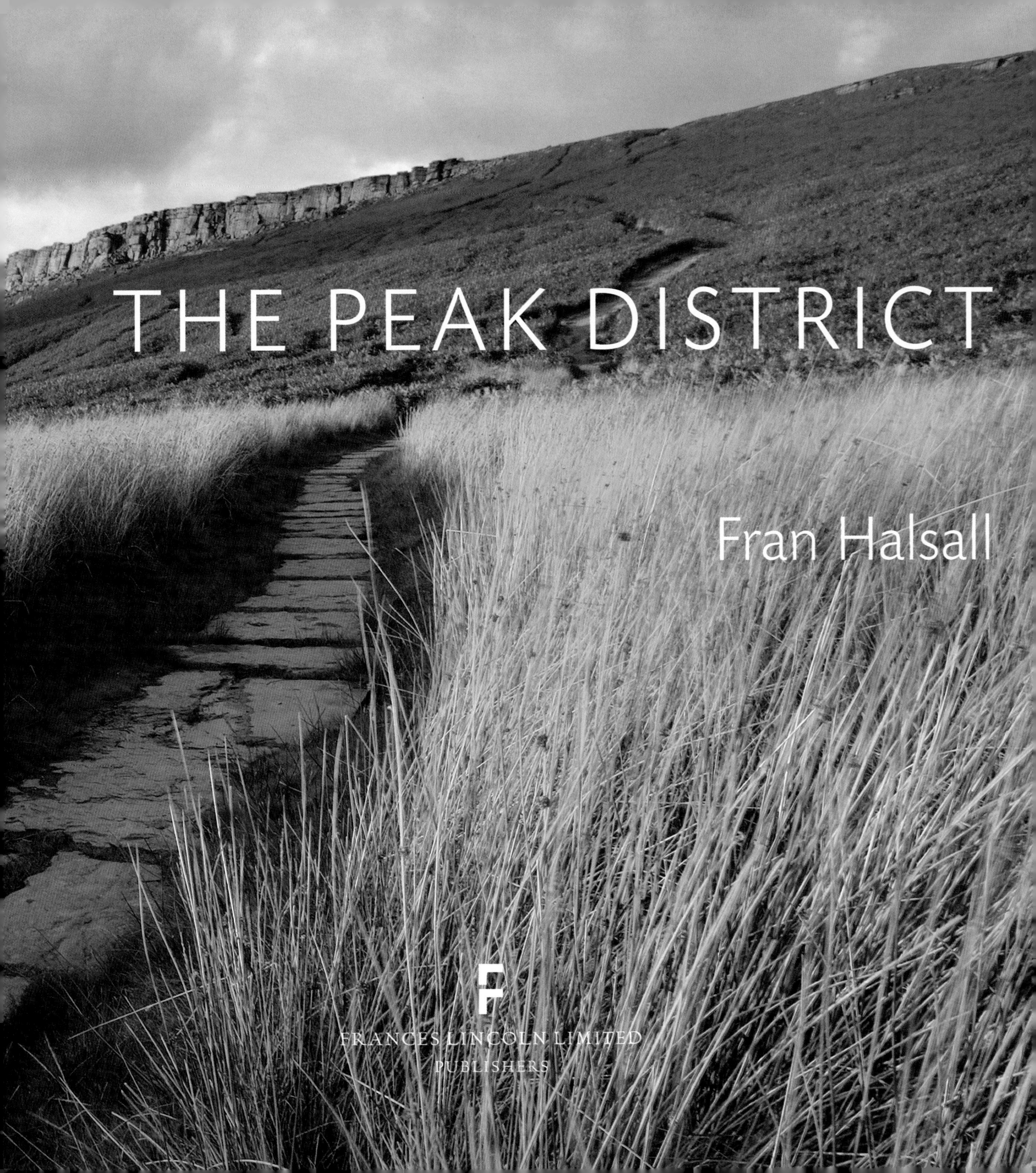

THE PEAK DISTRICT

Fran Halsall

F
FRANCES LINCOLN LIMITED
PUBLISHERS

For my grandfather. Thank you for introducing me to photography and for giving me my first camera.

Frances Lincoln Limited
4 Torriano Mews
Torriano Avenue
London NW5 2RZ
www.franceslincoln.com

The Peak District

First Frances Lincoln edition 2008

A catalogue record for this book is available from the British Library

ISBN 978-0-7112-2828-3

Printed and bound in Singapore

9 8 7 6 5 4 3 2 1

HALF TITLE PAGE: ***Old gateposts, Granby Wood, Upper Padley, Derbyshire, November 2006***
These gateposts mark a historical crossing point over Burbage Brook that runs through the middle of the wood. Now they sit idle and slightly askew, providing an inviting entrance to the mature broadleaf woodland.

TITLE PAGE: ***Stanage Edge, from Hooks Car, Derbyshire, October 2006***
Storm clouds frame the eastern approach to Stanage Edge; a sudden burst of golden light warms the autumnal moorland.

ABOVE: ***Upper Derwent Valley expanse, Derbyshire, November 2006***
From Derwent Edge the view south west is dominated by the Kinder plateau. Vivid sunsets such as this one, with unusual pink rays bursting forth from the horizon many minutes after sunset, are caused by smoke – from managed moorland burning – suspended in the atmosphere.

CONTENTS

Introduction 6
The Peak District National Park 8
Geology 11
Joint Character Areas 15
Managed Habitats 16
Woodland 21
Rivers and Reservoirs 24
Ancient Landmarks 28
Agriculture 31

The South West Peak 34
The White Peak 56
The Dark Peak 90

Further reading 126
Acknowledgments 126
About the photography 127
Technical notes 128

INTRODUCTION

The Peak Park is a region managed by the Peak District National Park Authority (PDNPA) in the interests of conservation, the upkeep of the landscape's features and economy and the promotion of responsible enjoyment of the countryside. It works in collaboration with organisations such as the National Trust, which owns 12.5 per cent of the land, and English Heritage, which maintains many ancient sites and historical features. English Nature has designated 30 per cent of the Peak Park as Sites of Special Scientific Interest (SSSIs) because of nationally important examples of flora, fauna and geology.

Its title inspires ideas of mountainous ranges and snow-capped summits but this image is not strictly accurate. The high points of Kinder Scout and Bleaklow are all over 600 m above sea level and technically qualify as mountains, but they are characteristically flat plateaux without a peak in sight. The region's many high hills more than make up for the lack of classic peaks. All shapes and sizes can be seen spanning parts of several counties: Derbyshire, Staffordshire, South and West Yorkshire, Cheshire and Greater Manchester. There are a few variations on the story of how the area became to be so-called, but it is generally agreed that it refers to the seventh-century Anglo-Saxon tribe known as the 'Peacsaetna' or 'Dwellers of the Peak'. 'The Peak' or 'The Peaks' are common corruptions in general use. The 'Peak District' is a broader description of the geographical area, within which the borders of the Peak Park fall.

My passion for the Peak Park arose from an appreciation of the uncluttered scenery, which started when I was doing my Fine Art degree at Manchester Metropolitan University. I found myself wanting to escape from the urban situation, and that led to my rediscovery of the natural space on my doorstep. Towards the end of my degree, I drew upon this region as the main inspiration for my image-making. With camera in tow, I began to document my reactions, recording changes – how the cyclical growth of vegetation colours the landscape – capturing the moods inspired by restless weather and observing the nature of shifting light. I gained a better understanding of the evolving relationship mankind has with this fragile environment, as both custodian and user of its many resources.

Many areas of the Peak Park are well-trodden and photographed. It is easy to see why: from the first images I took on film in this area in 2001, I knew I was going to have a long relationship with this rich and diverse locale. In 2004 I bought my first digital SLR camera – the Canon 10D – and from that moment it went everywhere with me. All the photographs in this book have been taken since that time. In 2006 I began using the Canon 5D digital SLR. Most photographs are the result of revisiting a site to capture the scene in the right conditions. Others are chance encounters: being in the right place at the right time. This collection records changing atmospheres and, as I got to know the area better, the descriptive details that tell the story. Using strong elements in my compositions, such as distinctive rocks, hills, trees, water, ancient monuments and so on, help to define the image and provide a context.

Subsequently, I have come to see how much humans have influenced the view. Great swathes of trees have been cleared for agriculture, leaving a few pockets of ancient woodland, and have been selectively replanted with conifers for logging. It has been flooded with reservoirs, quarried for rocks, mined for minerals and been traversed over its entire surface, leaving visible scars. This is all part of the long history of a landscape evolving in tandem with man's activities. Some of the most poignant examples of this relationship are the stone monuments dating from the Neolithic and Bronze Age periods, which provide tangible evidence of ancient land use. Traces of human relics on this landscape, the rocks beneath our feet, the rivers and tracks that intersect the terrain all provide the substance of my photographs.

This book contains approximately 150 images, which allows for the coverage of a range of sites. However, it would require a gargantuan book to take in every aspect of the Peak Park. For this reason I had to exclude many photographs from my initial selection. Two overriding factors have influenced my decisions: firstly I was guided by the relative importance of a location; secondly I wished to concentrate on especially significant places in some detail. For this reason several images have been included from one area. The narrative is written from the perspective of seeing the links between the landscape's aesthetic quality and knowing the story behind its appearance. By concentrating on the features of the Peak Park that have inspired my interest and fuelled my photography, I hope to pass on a passion for experiencing and conserving this magnificent environment.

THE PEAK DISTRICT NATIONAL PARK

Kinder Scout, Woolpacks and water, Derbyshire, December 2006
It is easy to see the attraction of Kinder Scout for walkers. The ascent is challenging and at the top one is rewarded with an intriguing variety of sandstone formations and an epic view. The group of boulders known as the Woolpacks sits on Kinder's southern flank. The overcast weather conditions seen here are a suitably forbidding setting for this remote and windswept location.

Environments such as the Peak Park are a precious resource. The world becomes ever more populated and the grab for the planet's natural wealth is consuming all in its path. This is why it is important to celebrate achievements such as the world's National Parks. Thanks to the foresight of a few, I can – along with many others like me – still enjoy the pleasure of wandering in open country and unspoilt places. My photographs are testament to the ceaseless inspiration that I draw from this landscape. The 1,424 square km of the country's central 'lungs', situated at the Pennine's southern tip, are hopefully forever protected from the more destructive and encroaching elements of civilisation.

The initial drive to designate the Peak Park as a National Park was inspired by early fears that the industrial towns surrounding it would spread to engulf this green heartland. The problem was compounded by the mechanisation of limestone quarrying, which became so efficient at extracting stone that it was eating away large areas of the White Peak's hills at an alarming rate. The Peak Park's boundary reflects the prevalence of quarrying locations. Towns such as Buxton, and other areas that have many of these sites, were excluded from the park in recognition of the fact that this industry is an essential part of the local economy and that it needed to continue where already established. It was hoped that by placing these sites outside the park's perimeter, it would prevent further quarrying within the park. This aim has been only partially successful.

People have always wanted to walk in the countryside but there have been historical problems in achieving this ambition. The flat-topped mountain of Kinder Scout became a focus for the disenchanted, the overworked and the unemployed of the cities lying within reach of its slopes. In 1894 the opening of the

Hope Valley railway line made visiting it a realistic possibility for many people coming from Sheffield, Manchester and even further afield. However, when they tried to climb it, access was forcibly prevented by gamekeepers working on behalf of landowners who wished to maintain the open moorlands purely for grouse-shooting.

The establishment of the Hayfield and Kinder Scout Ancient Footpaths Association in 1876 promoted the idea of public access to private land, known as the 'right to roam'. They produced pamphlets based on the original footpaths, cart and droving routes that constituted the rights of way across this landscape. In the early 1930s, public discontent was expressed by the massing of 10,000 people at Winatts Pass and Cave Dale at Castleton to protest at the lack of progress.

All this gave momentum to the 400-plus ramblers who staged a mass trespass on Kinder Scout on 24th April 1932. A now legendary action that led to the imprisonment of five individuals, it articulated the passionate point behind this protest and brought the issue to the nation's attention. Meanwhile the conservation movement was gaining momentum globally. In America, Yellowstone had been designated a National Park as far back as 1872. Inspired by this new wave of environmentalism and the pressure of public opinion, the government passed legislation that made the Peak Park Britain's first National Park in 1951.

More recently, the passing of the Countryside and Rights of Way Act (CroW) has ensured that access to this vital environment is maintained for all. The mapping of considerable parts of the British Isles as designated Access Land was completed in October 2005. This is a privilege that should not be abused: with access comes the personal responsibility not to damage the environment. Although the majority of the Peak Park landscape is privately owned, there is excellent access to most of it. An impressive 2,500 km of public rights of way are in place across the region. Until the creation of the National Park the highest parts of the region, Kinder Scout and Bleaklow, covering areas of 40 square km and 100 square km respectively, had no public footpaths crossing them. The Pennine Way, opened in 1965 as the first long-distance footpath in Britain, unfolds across these lofty summits.

The PDNPA works hard to maintain a balance between the different interests involved in using the land's resources. Homes for communities – more than 38,000 people live within the park – roads, quarrying, forestry, massive reservoirs, agriculture, manufacturing, leisure and tourism. After Mount Fuji National Park in Japan, the Peak Park is the second most visited in the world. All this activity coexists in an environment that needs to be managed with care and consideration. Consequently, the Peak Park is not a natural landscape. Its varied use over the centuries has shaped what we see today.

Bleaklow Head, cairn and post, Derbyshire, February 2007

A cairn marks the highest point on the flat mountain top of Bleaklow. Achieving 633 m at the summit, it falls just short of the maximum height of neighbouring Kinder Scout at 636m. In this austere upland, the landmarks are infrequent. The Pennine Way is the only definite path through vast tracts of peat bog.

GEOLOGY

When I first started visiting the Peak Park, I was struck by the duality of its scenery. The foundation for this contrast is the variety of rocks. Put simply: it is a case of pale lowland limestone against dark upland sandstone. The more I explored, the more important it became to understand the geology that forms the backbone of my photographs. The undulations of the landscape, with its craggy worn surface and oddly sculpted outcrops, are an endlessly fascinating subject. Rocks reveal the character of the Earth and influence the vegetation that grows on its surface. From elevated viewpoints overlooking the lowlands so much can be seen. At an unhurried pace more in keeping with the cycles of nature, I can just perceive the slow passage of time unfolding on a geological scale.

The majority of rocks within the Peak Park are sedimentary and were formed in the Carboniferous period. The limestone core of the White Peak dates from the Early Carboniferous starting about 360 million years ago. The younger sandstones of the Dark Peak, which encircle the limestone in an upside-down horseshoe shape, date from the Late Carboniferous from around 320 million years ago. At the start of the Carboniferous period, Britain was a small part of a massive continent. Situated just south of the equator, the area now within the Peak Park developed in a shallow shelf sea.

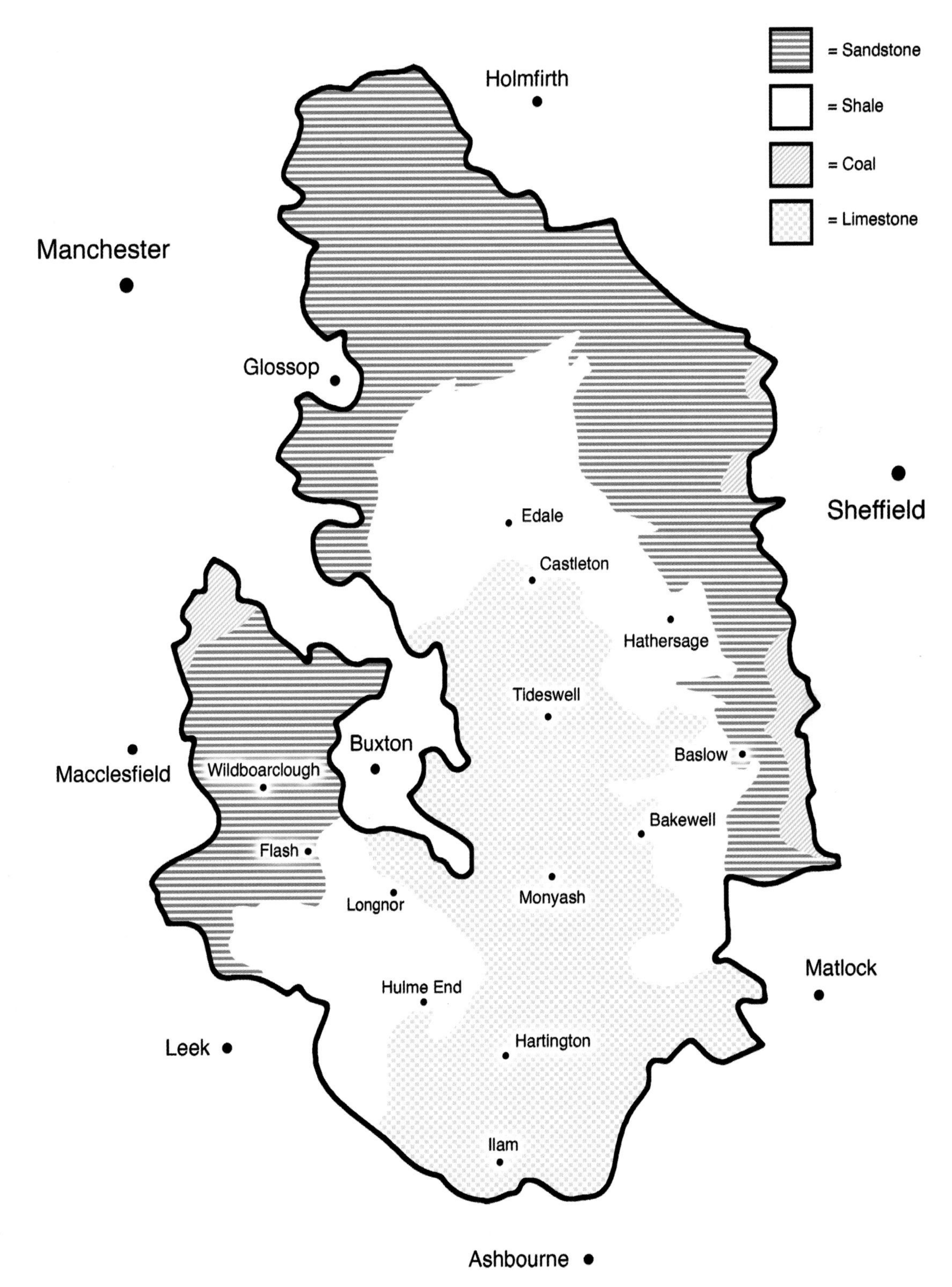

Early Carboniferous

Limestone is formed from the shells and skeletons of the sea creatures that once thrived in this warm clear water. When they died their calcium carbonate remains accumulated on the sea floor, building up layers of lime sand and lime mud that eventually formed limestone. Evidence of the richness of life from this period can be seen in the great variety of fossils preserved in the rock. In many places the limestone, lacking 'impurities' such as clays, is white. Elsewhere it appears in varying shades of grey.

Typical of the limestone dales are dry valleys that no longer contain streams. A dry valley can be a rocky gorge carved out long ago by massive flows of water or have grass-covered slopes cut by the more moderate action of streams. Dovedale is a fine example of limestone scenery where the valley floor has been cut down to the water table thus having a vigorous river running through it. The actions of this water can be seen in formations such as the Tissington Spires, which are eroded limestone pinnacles soaring up from the valley floor. The vegetation serves an essential role in maintaining the slopes beneath the spires, helping to resist the erosion that is seen in the boulder scree below.

Rainwater combined with carbon dioxide from the atmosphere and from soil forms weak carbonic acid that seeps into the groundwater. This widens the lines of weakness in the rock, dissolving the soluble limestone, which can cause underground streams to develop. In turn by eroding surrounding rocks, the streams carry boulders and pebbles which themselves cause more substantial erosion, leading eventually to the creation of large caves.

Tissington Spires, Dovedale, Derbyshire/Staffordshire, May 2006

Blue John Cavern, Canyon Passage, Castleton, Derbyshire March 2006

A view up into what was formerly the channel of an underground stream that has long-since vanished. Where water now flows over the surface of cave walls, crystalline calcium carbonate deposits leave formations known as flowstones. Pink colouration is caused by the presence of iron oxides; green algae grow where there is fixed lighting in the cave.

Bolehill Quarry, Longshaw Estate, Derbyshire, October 2006

Late Carboniferous

Subsequent layers of sand (quartz grains) and mud, borne down from northern mountains by an ancient river system, spread out over the limestone to form a broad delta in the sea. The sand and mud were buried and compacted under pressure to form layers of sandstones and clay rocks (often called shales). Some of the coarse-grained sandstones – commonly referred to as Millstone Grit, for which the region is famous – were quarried to make millstones from the post-medieval period until the nineteenth century. Coarse-grained sandstone containing waterworn pebbles is referred to as conglomeratic. There are several sandstones in the Peak Park referred to as 'grits', such as Chatsworth Grit. The sandstone uplands define the Dark Peak and the higher parts of the South West Peak.

The image above is from a rockface quarried at around the end of the nineteenth and beginning of the twentieth centuries, showing a red sandstone coloured by the presence of iron oxides. The now disused Bolehill Quarry was the source of the stone used in the construction of the Howden and the Derwent Reservoir Dams. It was part of a group of quarries on the East Moors of Derbyshire, centred on the villages of Baslow and Hathersage, which were particularly productive in the eighteenth and nineteenth centuries. Fast-growing birch trees have populated this quarry since it fell into disuse and softened the human impact on the landscape. Some of the Peak Park sandstone quarries are still active, such as those around Stanton Moor, providing a much sought-after building material. This inevitably leads to a conflict of interests between people representing the need to preserve the landscape and those who wish to use its resources.

The tough nature of sandstone is most evident in the escarpments (cliffs) of the East Moors. It contains natural, vertical breaks or joints, which allow collapses of large amounts of rock to produce faces that are nearly perpendicular, beneath which lie boulder-scattered slopes. The most famous example is Stanage Edge (see pages 108–9). On the surfaces above these escarpments, unusual rock outcrops known as tors can often be found. One of the best-known tors, the Wheel Stones on Derwent Moor (overleaf), show different layers of sandstone separated by partings referred to as bedding planes. These bands of rock, or strata, are of varying toughness and so are subject to different rates of erosion, resulting in the interesting patterns typical of exposed sandstone.

Shale is a fine-grained sedimentary rock formed from clay and mud particles. Areas of shale are found in many places in the Peak Park. Shale is generally fragile and is at risk of being weakened further by water seeping along bedding planes. This can result in dramatic landslips such as those at Mam Tor (see pages 110–11) and also Alport Castles (see page 124). At both sites the hill has fallen away leaving noticeable bands of rock devoid of vegetation.

Minerals

The spreading river delta was formed in tropical climate conditions, and was sometimes colonised by swamps, leading to the formation of extensive peats. Some of these peat layers were buried by later sediments and compacted to form coal seams, trapped between sandstone and shale layers. Coal was extracted on a small-scale from the 1600s onwards. Most seams were too thin to be very productive, but there are extensive workings in the Goyt Valley and in the ground west of Axe Edge. Some of the coal continued to be mined into the twentieth century.

The region is more usually associated with the extraction of lead ore (galena), started in the Roman era but ended some years ago. Many mineralised veins were worked in limestone in search of galena, which carried trace amounts of silver, but it was notoriously difficult to locate. In addition, there are other minerals associated with galena: calcite and fluorite being two commonly occurring types. The regional deposits of fluorite (calcium fluoride) are of national importance due to their high quality. Castleton has its own unique variety of fluorite called Blue John, known for its colour bands. Blue John is used for ornamental purposes and is sold in the village's many gift shops, its rarity helping to popularise Castleton as an early tourist destination.

Due to the toxicity of lead, mining has left contaminated environments in its wake. Few plants will tolerate these conditions, but leadwort and mountain pansy thrive on the abandoned spoil heaps known as rakes. Lime has been quarried in the White Peak since Roman times and limekilns still litter the landscape. Nowadays massive quantities are produced for industrial applications, agriculture, road-building and cement manufacture, forming a major part of the local economy.

The Wheel Stones, Derwent Moor, Upper Derwent Valley, Derbyshire, November 2006

JOINT CHARACTER AREAS

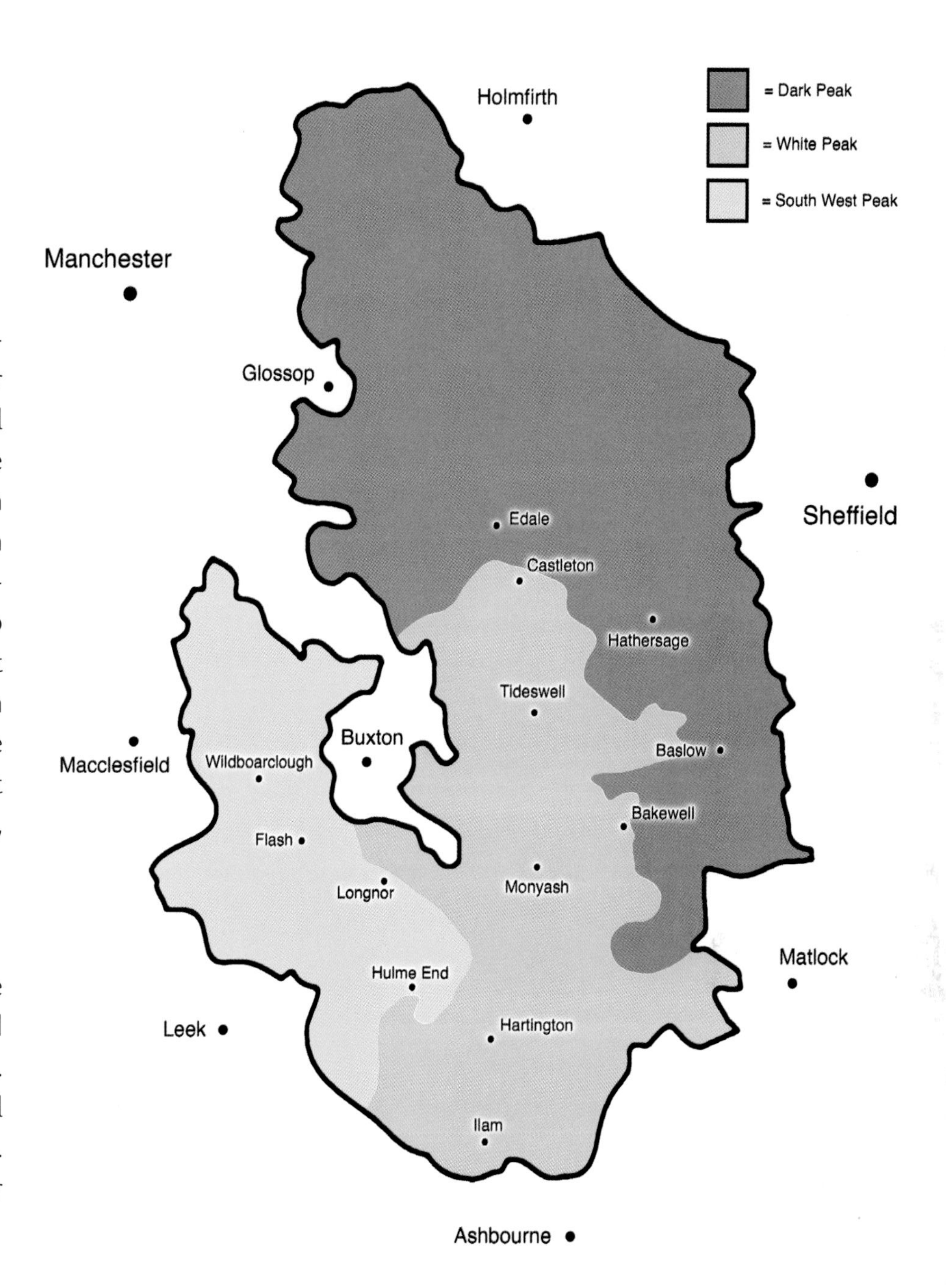

Previously the Peak Park was split into two geological zones: the White and Dark Peaks, the former founded on limestone, the latter on sandstone and shale. However, this does not accurately reflect the ecology of the region. It helps for those working in environment conservation to be able to distinguish between various habitats. Consequently recent reclassification by Natural England has resulted in a new map being drawn up that divides England into 159 'Joint Character Areas' (JCAs) based on the features, both natural and man-made, defining the appearance of the landscape. Following this methodology, the area is best described as consisting of three zones: the South West, White and Dark Peaks.

South West Peak
The South West Peak is formed from sandstone, shale and coal seams. The remains of the short-lived coal mining industry can be seen around the village of Flash. The uplands are mostly covered in heather dominated moorland, blanket bog and some wooded cloughs. There are some grasslands and hay meadows at lower altitude. Sheep, cattle and dairy farming prevail here.

White Peak
The White Peak is characterised by a limestone landscape with flat plateaux, narrow dales and caves. The rivers, some of which are seasonal, have a major impact on the landscape. Its vegetation is made up of grasslands, hay meadows and broadleaf woodland. Large-scale limestone quarries and intensive dairy farming affect the landscape's appearance.

Dark Peak
The Dark Peak is known for its sandstone escarpments (cliff edges) topped by either blanket bog or heather moorland, and exposed shale/sandstone areas. Fast flowing streams descend into broad valleys, sometimes containing man-made reservoirs, often with coniferous tree plantations. Semi-natural woodlands can be found in cloughs. Isolated farms exist on rough, sheep-grazing pasture.

MANAGED HABITATS

The Peak Park's diversity is determined not only by the variety of exposed rocks, but by the contrasting vegetation that paints the landscape with many hues. Vast heather moorlands under open skies overlook gentle grasslands surrounded by hills, providing a dynamic spectrum of colour to photograph. It is this scenery for which the Peak Park is celebrated and universally known, and yet both of these habitats – which could be considered the zenith of nature's creative force – are in fact heavily altered by man's traditional use of the land. The future of these iconic environments is dependent upon careful management.

Heather Moorland & Blanket Bogs

Heather Moorland

Moorlands are usually found on hillsides and plateaux above 250 m. Initially they appear to be entirely natural, occurring as they often do in distant locations. However they result from the systematic clearance of woodland by early farmers to make room for crops and for grazing animals. The colder and wetter climate dating from 600 BC prevented trees regrowing; over time both factors contributed to a decrease in soil fertility as nutrients were leached from it by water.

Morridge Moor, birch among heather, Staffordshire, August 2005

Birch trees, often situated in isolated clumps on the heath, serve as a reminder of what the upland landscape would have looked like before clearance. Heather is the typical vegetation on thinner peat or mineral soils. The dominant variety growing in the Peak Park, common heather, is often referred to as ling. It is this that accounts for purple carpets of flowers in late summer, and is easily distinguished from the larger-flowered bell heather, which blooms slightly earlier. The bright foliage of crowberry and bilberry punctuate the groundcover in places. Fast-growing bracken has spread from lowland and woodland areas, and is rapidly taking over the moors at the expense of other plant varieties.

The heath is home to the red grouse, the most iconic of all the birds in the area. This bird is hunted seasonally, and efforts are made to boost the population by deliberately burning selected areas of moorland to remove dead scrub and encourage new plant shoots, important in their diet. This illustrates the ambiguous issues surrounding the need to both protect and profit from this landscape. One is usually made aware of a nearby grouse by hearing its distinctive call or witnessing one of their sudden aerial territorial displays. Other notable bird species populating the moors include seasonal visitors such as golden plover and curlew and predators such as merlin and hen harriers. As the last high point before the descent into lowland Britain, the Dark Peak marks the southern limit of the mountain hare's range.

Blanket Bogs

Extensive areas of the South West and Dark Peak's uplands are covered in blanket peat bog at least 50 cm deep. Exposed uplands suffer high winds, frost and heavy rains, causing erosion of the peat layers where vegetation has been removed. This occurs as a result of overgrazing by sheep, over-used footpaths, and accidental fires that can be so severe they consume the peat itself. Sphagnum mosses and lichens that formerly protected the surface of the peat have often been killed off by acid rain. Although sulphur dioxide emissions from the coal-fired Industrial Revolution, the original cause of acid rain, are at their lowest level since the nineteenth century, there are still large quantities of hydrocarbons in the atmosphere and nitrogen oxides being emitted from cars, pollutants that increase the levels of peat acidity. This harsh environment supports a limited range of vegetation, although some plants such as the common cotton grass – a type of sedge – are prolific (see page 54).

The otherworldly landscape of Bleaklow (overleaf), the surface of which consists of blanket bog, is a potent example of the need for active conservation. The fragile terrain at the summit is now classed as desert. A recent initiative saw 22 km of fencing erected to prevent sheep grazing the grasses and heather vital to the stability of the peat mounds.

The preservation of moorland ecosystems is critical on a global scale, because it has such a limited range. Up to 15 per cent of the world's blanket bogs and a staggering 75 per cent

New growth on peat mounds, Bleaklow, Derbyshire, February 2007

of the world's heather moorland are in the British Isles. This is especially relevant to the current debate on controlling carbon emissions. Peat bogs form natural sinks, containing more carbon than all the woodlands of the British Isles and France combined.

Grasslands & Hay Meadows

The Peak Park hosts grassland and hay meadows containing an array of wildflowers of the kind once common across lowland Britain. The variety of colour they provide is especially noticeable next to the vivid green of fertilised farmland.

Calcareous Grassland

This kind of habitat is typically found on the slopes and crags of the limestone dales where the soil is thin and alkaline. It is considered the most species-rich of the different types of grassland. Small lime-loving plants populate areas of grass kept short by grazing sheep and cattle, an activity that has been practised in this region for centuries. If these locations were not grazed, trees such as hazel and hawthorn would quickly repopulate the area at the expense of floral diversity. This type of environment is particularly at risk from aggregate quarrying, many sites having already been damaged or wiped out. However, if disused quarries are

properly restored, the habitat can recover. Quarrying companies working with the PDNPA are making sure that these sites have the best chance of becoming productive again.

Acid Grassland

When the underlying rock consists of sandstone and/or shale soil becomes acid. Species such as devil's-bit scabious, harebell and betony can be found where springs emerge and on damp ground. There are few examples of this type of habitat in the Peak Park.

Common spotted orchid, Brierlow Bar, Derbyshire, June 2004

This orchid is growing remarkably close to an active limestone quarry, in conditions similar to its native habitat in calcareous grasslands, where it grows prolifically in the summer months. Other varieties, such as the early purple orchid, also feature strongly in this locality alongside plants such as cowslip, lady's bedstraw and wild thyme. Several species of butterfly inhabit these areas including the dark green fritillary, common blue and meadow brown.

Wetland Meadow

Few outposts are left of this kind of waterlogged habitat. Marsh marigolds, soft rushes and meadowsweet can be found at the margins of some rivers. Many marshes have been drained to increase grazing land

Neutral Grassland

Where there is a deep layer of soil it is unaffected by the rock beneath, resulting in soils that have a neutral pH value. Ox-eye daisies, hay rattle and meadow clover are abundant in this type of habitat, which is the most commonly occurring grassland in the region. The hay rattle derives its name from the sound the mature seed pod makes when shaken. In land managed as a hay meadow this was a sign that the field was ready for harvesting.

Hay Meadows

The long grasses of hay meadows are not just aesthetically pleasing; they can support up to fifty plant species per square metre, forming a key part of the Peak Park's ecology. These habitats result from traditional farming practices, where livestock are removed from grazing meadows in spring allowing grass and wildflowers to grow and set seed. In late summer the meadow is cut down to make hay for feeding animals in winter. Tall vegetation is the perfect hiding place for breeding birds, the Peak Park having significant populations of the globally threatened skylark, grey partridge and twite. It also provides a home for the brown hare and many butterflies.

Hay meadows are particularly under threat from intensive farming, which has repercussions for biodiversity. The centuries-old practice of haymaking is being replaced by silage production, which means that fields are cut more often, allowing less time for grass and wildflower growth. Longer periods of grazing by livestock also impact on the growth cycle.

These changes are exacerbated by atmospheric pollution and add up to a sharp reduction in the percentage and quality of these habitats, the loss felt most keenly in land devoted to dairy production.

Some of the best places to see the remaining grasslands and hay meadows within the Peak Park are the National Nature Reserves (NNRs). Derbyshire Dales NNR, maintained by English Nature, incorporates the dales of Cressbrook, Hay, Lathkill, Long and Monk's, all of which are limestone habitats; Dovedale NNR, established in October 2006, is the responsibility of the National Trust and is considered to be one of the finest examples of calcareous grassland in Britain, hosting fine ash woodlands on its slopes; Biggin Dale NNR is also managed by the National Trust; Deep Dale NNR, managed by Plantlife, is transformed in spring by the contrasting flowers of yellow cowslips and early purple orchids, and its steep slopes are covered in lime-loving plants throughout the summer.

Hay meadow, Reapsmoor, Staffordshire, May 2007

WOODLAND

Trees define the seasons: the annual renewal of broadleaf woodland is marked by acid greens in spring, while those of summer are vibrant, and autumn foliage radiates fiery colours. The stark winter silhouette of the leafless tree is a powerful reminder of nature's cyclical pattern, a pause before the warmth of spring. Isolated trees are a recurring motif in my images, acting as distinctive landmarks. I like to immerse myself in woodlands, where an unspoken connection exists between the present and long-vanished primeval times. With its dappled light and heavy shade, woodland can be technically difficult to photograph, but is a rewarding pursuit.

After the last ice age Britain was colonised by extensive birch woods that were well adapted to the harsh climate. A rise in temperature starting around 10,000 ago years led to birch being replaced by other broadleaf trees such as oak, elm and hazel. Birch trees persist in upland areas where they are a common sight on moorlands alongside rowan and oak. The downy birch (see Eaglestone Flat, page 90) is especially well adapted to nutrient-poor upland soil. The sessile oak is more often found in the uplands and, as a result of the environment, can become gnarled and twisted. In places such as Yarncliffe Wood (see page 97) the sessile oaks that make up the majority of trees were planted over 100 years ago and were used for making charcoal to feed the Sheffield iron industry's furnaces.

The common oak is the most widespread British broadleaf tree – in the Peak Park usually found in the lower areas. In the illustration overleaf, a solitary specimen overlooks verdant summer pasture high above the Manifold Valley. Isolated trees such as this are survivors of woodland that once covered the plateau. In the Peak Park most remaining trees are found in deeply wooded valleys. A mature oak, growing up to 40 m, can support over 300 different species of insects, forming an integral part of the ecosystem. They are symbolic of endurance as it is not uncommon for them to live up to 1,000 years, even after the centre of the trunk has rotted away. The oak is held in such high esteem that it is a national symbol.

Trees have many functions: first providing extensive habitats; second protecting the soil from erosion and flooding. Finally, and most significantly for us, they take in carbon dioxide and release breathable oxygen into the atmosphere. It is staggering to think that but for the intervention of man, particularly clearance associated with farming, as much as 80 per cent of Britain would be covered in woods. Today England has one of the lowest percentages of woodland cover in Europe. The PDNPA and the National Trust work hard to maintain existing woods, planting new trees and encouraging other landowners to do the same. The areas that are now highly-prized heather moorlands, calcareous grasslands and hay meadows were once wooded, so there is a delicate balance to maintain between these different environments.

There is little left to remind one of the original 'wildwood' of past millennia, as most of Britain's forests are only a few hundred years old. Folk memories of wood spirits remain, variously known as Pan, Puck, Robin Goodfellow, the Green Man and Hob Hurst – the local denizen of sacred places. Meadow Place Wood in Lathkill Dale NNR is one of the rare places where woodland that has changed little in the last 8,000 years can be found. Beech, ash and elm predominate providing

Backlit common oak, Wetton, Staffordshire, May 2006

shady conditions for hart's tongue and male ferns, wood sorrel and yellow archangel growing among rotting tree trunks and deep leaf litter.

The White Peak has the largest concentration of ash woodlands in the British Isles, among these are surviving fragments of ancient woods that can be traced on maps dating back to 1600. The prevalence of ash in the limestone dales is reflected in names such as the village of Monyash – probably derived from 'many ashes', which is sited near the now disappeared One Ash village. Ash woods, which commonly include hazel and small- and large-leaved limes, have a long history of being coppiced for fuel. Ash, or sometimes oak, was chosen for the traditional winter yule log, burnt to symbolise the returning sun. In British folklore the ash is associated with healing properties, parts of the tree being used for medicines: for example newborn babies were given the sap to aid strength.

Britain's wooded landscape underwent a dramatic change in the early twentieth century. The Forestry Commission was set up in 1919 to protect and regenerate Britain's woods, establishing new forests including the conifer plantations of the Peak

Park. The prevailing view was that open moors were waste-lands, so were planted with conifers for timber production. Founding large areas of non-native coniferous species such as larch, pine and spruce causes problems. Because they grow so close to each other, plantations are dark environments with limited wildlife. However, birds such as crossbills, coal tits and goldcrests thrive in tree-tops.

Pines at the margins of Derwent Reservoir are typical of the trees dominating this valley, although there are some pockets of broadleaf trees. Brackens form the majority of ground cover in these plantations. In the Upper Derwent Valley, Severn Trent Water and the Forestry Commission own 829 hectares and 430 hectares of woodland respectively. When planted on the sides of reservoirs, conifers have the additional purpose of preventing peaty surface soil from sliding into the drinking water.

LEFT: ***Meadow Place Wood, Lathkill Dale, Derbyshire, May 2007***
BELOW: ***Pines, Upper Derwent Valley, Derbyshire, September 2006***

RIVERS AND RESERVOIRS

Water is very appealing: reflective when still and dynamic when tumbling down edges as waterfalls. Rivers are the most powerful erosive force on land, winding round, down and through hills forming ravines and caves as they go. The floral diversity and interesting geology typical of the region have been shaped by the constant presence of water since the glacial melts after the last ice age. Rivers define a place and mark boundaries, both real and imagined. The hills of the Peak Park attract high rainfall so many rivers spread across its surface, some finding their way into huge reservoirs. In spring, seasonal downpours swell the rivers and bring life to the valleys.

The River Wye enters the Peak Park at Chee Dale, a deep limestone gorge featuring dense ash woodland. As it winds below the impressive Chee Tor it nourishes marginal plants such as the ubiquitous butterbur seen here. The Wye is associated with its very own water deity, Arnemetia, sometimes known as Anu. Her sacred spring is where the river emerges inside Poole's Cavern, Buxton. Votive deposits at the site date the veneration to as early as the first century AD, such offerings continued until the fourth century AD. So important was her cult that when the Romans arrived to claim the settlement in AD 78 they called it Aquae Arnemetiae, or the 'Waters of Arnemetia'. This devotion follows a widespread pattern of

River Wye, Chee Dale, Derbyshire, May 2007

ancient belief that saw many rivers, waterfalls, springs and pools linked with guardian spirits, an acknowledgment of water's life-sustaining role and its perceived regenerative effects.

The subsequent Christianisation of this ritual led to Arnemetia becoming identified with St Anne, who has a well dedicated to her in the centre of Buxton, away from the natural setting of the cave. The well, complete with a statue of St Anne and her daughter Mary, is the focus for the town's well-dressing celebrations. This custom has an obscure origin and was initially banned by the Christian church along with other forms of pagan worship. In its current decorative floral incarnation, it is an expression of gratitude for the purity of the water drawn from well and is celebrated throughout the villages and towns of the Peak Park. Historically the well-flowering – as it is sometimes known – is unique to Derbyshire and Staffordshire. It first appeared in the historical record at Tissington village after the inhabitants escaped an outbreak of the Black Death.

The River Derwent starts life on remote rain-saturated moorlands, like many other rivers in the Peak Park. It rises at Swain's Greave on Howden Moor from where it flows for 80 km before it joining the River Trent near Derby. It is the largest river in the Peak Park, lending its name to the entire valley, and is dammed in its upper reaches to form the Howden, Derwent and Ladybower Reservoirs. The Howden dam was built in 1912, followed by the Derwent dam in 1916. Both phases of Ladybower, a vast reservoir split into two by the Ashopton Bridge, were completed by the mid-1940s. The surrounding cities benefit from a water supply of 450 million litres per day, the combined total from all the reservoirs in the Peak Park. They were a controversial project when first proposed, but many visitors now admire these immense bodies of water. The reservoirs are an integral part of the Dark Peak landscape.

The rivers Dove and Manifold emerge within a short distance of each other on the sandstone uplands of Axe Edge. Their upper reaches flow roughly in parallel, separated only by high ground, until they reach Longnor village. When these rivers hit limestone country, their influence on the surrounding geology creates some of the finest scenery in the White Peak.

The River Manifold rises at Flash Head (see pages 44–5), from where it flows for 19 km before it joins the Dove near the base of Thorpe Cloud (see page 56). The river is reduced to a mere puddle during its 'dry' season because the limestone in this part of the valley is riddled with subterranean caves, as seen in the photograph taken at Dafar Bridge overleaf. In reality, it has gone underground only to reappear further down the valley at Ilam. The changes in this river are unpredictable. I took this photograph standing in the riverbed; only two weeks later it was a torrent once more, later drying out again for summer and autumn. The River Hamps is the Manifold's main tributary.

The River Dove's origins begin at Dove Head (see pages 46–7) on the border between Derbyshire and Staffordshire. It

continues for 72 km before it empties into the River Trent near Burton, defining the county boundary throughout most of its course. In contrast to the raging torrent that carved out ravines, isolated reefs and created a broad flat valley, the Dove is now relatively narrow and gentle. It is thought to take its name from 'Dubo', the Norse word for dark, a reference to the water's steely-grey colour in winter.

ABOVE: ***Reflected clouds, Derwent Reservoir, Upper Derwent Valley, Derbyshire, October 2006***

RIGHT: ***Dafar Bridge, dry River Manifold, near Wetton, Staffordshire, May 2006***

ANCIENT LANDMARKS

Gib Hill barrow, near Monyash, Derbyshire, April 2007

The Peak Park's ancient heritage fascinates me. Observing the expanse of time between the construction of ritual monuments and the present provides a link to a remote age of the landscape's past. The first stone circle I photographed was the fine example of Arbor Low near Monyash. Even under the overcast sky at our first encounter, it felt momentous. Then I started reading about this and other monuments and I became captivated. In documenting them, I am trying to translate the powerful sense of place into my photographs. To do this accurately, I make every effort to record the site with the right angle of illumination and in the appropriate season. Because they often have a low profile they can prove difficult to photograph, so my challenge has been to find the best approach for each location.

Since its earliest occupation, different cultures have made their mark on the region's landscape. Neolithic people were the first settlers, following on from the nomadic Mesolithic hunter-gatherers of the previous period. They enjoyed a much gentler climate than that of today, which encouraged the settlement of early farming communities on productive land. Where these people made their homes, they erected monuments, some of which survive today. The first of these were barrows for the ceremonial burial of the dead, followed by chambered cairns and subsequently the large henge monuments of the White Peak. Neolithic communities made their religious sites from the exposed rocks of the earth itself, perhaps solely because it was so readily available. Whatever the reason, because they chose long-lasting stone we can witness

the results even if we cannot fully grasp their ritual significance.

The period including the Late Neolithic and Early Bronze Age saw the construction of more than 500 round barrows. First impressions are that Gib Hill is a prominent example of this type of monument, but closer inspection shows it to be a Bronze Age round barrow superimposed on a Neolithic long barrow. In spite of it being somewhat overshadowed by the adjacent Arbor Low, Gib Hill was the first ceremonial feature at this location. A typical barrow is constructed from large stone slabs, drystone walling and topped by an earthen mound. Many excavated barrows have been found to contain skeletons; ceramic urns in others hold cremated remains. Sometimes these appear in conjunction with cairns which range from simple conical collections of stones placed on the burial mound, or can extend to the complex structure of a chambered cairn, consisting of upright stones and a cap-stone defining a tomb space. (see Five Wells, pages 78–9) Not every stone cairn has a ritual purpose: some are piles left behind after clearing rocks from a field in order to grow crops or graze animals, and many of these are also ancient in origin.

On a warm spring evening the setting sun casts a gentle glow across the lichen-encrusted surface of Arbor Low's recumbent limestone slabs.

Arbor Low, looking north west, near Monyash, Derbyshire, May 2005

Although many people assume they have fallen down, because most circles feature upright stones, there is a lack of evidence to indicate the builders' intentions. The low angle of the sun reveals the earthen ring bank, known as a henge, in deep shadow. It was built to define the sacred space, enhanced by cove stones included at the heart of the structure to offer privacy for the site's users. Arbor Low dates from the late Neolithic period and was a large ritual site, probably visited from many surrounding settlements. In the Peak Park, the henge type of monument is found only in the White Peak.

In the later Neolithic/Early Bronze Age, monument construction shifted towards smaller stone circles. These sites are closely associated with individual communities and are frequently sited on the higher plateaux of Derbyshire's East Moors. During this period at least twenty-six stone circles were built, typical of these being the Nine Stones Close on Harthill Moor (see page 66) and the Nine Ladies of Stanton Moor (see page 71). From modern observations of these sacred sites, it is understood that sometimes the builders deliberately aligned these structures with the cycles of the sun and moon, a relationship that can still be seen today. Looking west from Nine Stones Close towards Robin Hood's Stride outcrop a short distance away is where the midsummer moonrise emerges between its two towers. Knowledge of these seasonal measurements would have been especially significant to early farmers, perhaps helping them to sow and harvest their crops at the optimum time.

The partially wooded plain at the top of Gardom's Edge on the East Moors above Baslow village reveals a long and varied history of human influence. Neolithic field enclosures show that early farming existed at the site, Bronze Age cairns and the remains of Iron Age dwellings confirming that occupation continued for many hundred of years. One of the most vivid examples of the relationship between early communities and the landscape exists at a spot slightly away from the edge. A petroglyph carved into a sandstone slab sits at the fringes of birch woodland. Discovered as recently as the 1960s, the rock carving already showed signs of severe weathering. To avert further deterioration a fibreglass cast was put in place over the top of the original, the photograph showing the convincing copy. The meaning of cup and ring marks is a matter of much debate. Are they art? Were they functional? Petroglyphs are associated with ancient monuments throughout the world, occurring in many cultures, exciting much interest and speculation. However, from a modern viewpoint it is impossible to know for certain the reason behind their creation.

Petroglyph, Gardom's Edge, Derbyshire, February 2007.

AGRICULTURE

Scattered across the Peak Park is the evidence of how people have managed the landscape for thousands of years. This takes a variety of forms, including linear stonewalls and the various shapes of barns and farmsteads. There are also more subtle indications: low earthworks – half-hidden by moorland vegetation – revealing ancient land use. Then there is the overall lack of trees resulting from clearance started in the Mesolithic period as a means of encouraging animals to come to a specific location to make hunting easier. Human activity continues to shape the 'nature' of this landscape, leaving no area unaffected and, as such, forms an integral part of my documentation of the area.

Neolithic people were the first farmers, starting crop cultivation and rearing animals. Initially they were nomadic; the limestone plateaux and sandstone uplands being ideal for summer grazing, while heavily wooded valleys provided shelter and food in winter. Eventually groups settled in specific places probably near existing barrows, a relationship that may well have reinforced the 'land rights' of a tribal group. Some woodland was coppiced for fuel and timber but other trees were cleared for crop-growing, animal-grazing and supplying building material.

In the Iron Age, the weather worsened and soil quality deteriorated causing people to leave the higher parts of the Peak Park, possibly in favour of limestone plateaux and sheltered valleys. Some isolated farms persevere in this often windy and wet environment, such as the one at Morridge Top. Although the buildings are usually only a few hundred years old, they may be built on sites used for millennia. The conditions will not support the growing of arable crops, so rearing livestock is the most important farming activity. Most grazing animals in the Peak Park are sheep with cows accounting for the rest. Typically sheep and beef cattle are raised on the rougher pastures of the Dark and South West Peaks, whereas the White Peak plateax are used for rearing dairy cattle.

Isolated farms and hamlets were probably abandoned in favour of the larger post-Roman settlements which eventually developed into today's villages. From the tenth century land around villages was farmed as open fields by the whole

Morridge Top Farm, near Flash, Staffordhire, August 2006

community, rented free from the lord of the manor in exchange for their labour on his own land. The land was divided into long and narrow strips, good and bad being distributed equally; a system which can still be seen clustered around many villages. Repeated ploughing of strip fields in one direction has left undulating traces in the ground known as ridge and furrow. They are easiest to see when the sun is low and shadows are long.

The walls seen from the vantage point of Curbar Edge have a jumbled and seemingly arbitrary layout. The Peak Park's drystone walls have come to symbolise the character of this landscape. Built from local rock, in limestone areas they appear as white lines against lush green fields – and in sandstone districts their various earthy colours often blend in with the upland's coarser vegetation. Fields began to be enclosed with stone in the medieval period, usually following the boundaries of existing strip divisions (see Foolow, page 82). In post-medieval times many dwellings were replaced by the stone buildings that characterise Peak Park villages today.

Enclosure continued at a gradual pace and was eventually subject to enclosure awards in the eighteenth and nineteenth centuries, when parliamentary acts were introduced to improve the output of open, arable and grazing fields. These later walls were built ruler-straight in accordance with prepared plans. Because much of the land in the Peak Park was already walled strip fields, these enclosures often took in the upper reaches of farmland and areas that were considered 'commons'; a cause for complaint among farmers reliant on them for grazing livestock. On the ground

Field enclosures, Curbar, Derbyshire, November 2005

it is difficult to see the difference between earlier and later walled enclosures.

Many field barns date from the post-medieval period and include small structures, as seen here, erected purely for the storage of food for cattle. The larger, two-storey buildings were used to keep harvested grasses in a hayloft above, which could then easily be fed to sheltering animals below (see pages 62–3). Barns were needed when fields were separated from the farmstead, thus saving the labour of moving cattle and food back and forth. Changes in modern farming practices are highlighted by the ruinous state of many barns – they simply have no place in more intensive agriculture. A few of the larger ones have been converted for use as camping barns, but most have been abandoned.

The pattern of farming established over generations has changed in recent years. Demands imposed by intensive agricultural production have forced many farmers to adapt in order to survive. Diversification has included organic, local and specialist foods production, and converting parts of farms into holiday cottages. Because of concerns over the loss of habitats in the Environmentally Sensitive Areas (ESAs) of the Dark and South West Peaks, farmers can obtain grants to manage their land for conservation from the Ministry of Agriculture. Outside the ESAs, the Countryside Stewardship Scheme encourages farmers and other landowners to conserve ecologically and historically important sites.

Ruined field barn, Longnor, Staffordshire, April 2004

THE SOUTH WEST PEAK

Blake Mere, Morridge Moor, Staffordshire, December 2005
This reputedly bottomless pool is in a hollow on Morridge Moor, North Staffordshire. Although marked as Blake Mere on Ordnance Survey maps, locally it is known as Mermaid Pool, stemming from the legend of a vengeful mermaid who drags men to a watery death around the stroke of midnight.

Dawn temperature inversion, Morridge Moor, Staffordshire, January 2006
A spectacular flush of lilac light catches mist rolling up on to the moorlands from Leek. The brown bog-vegetation is a featureless mass disappearing into engulfing mist.

ABOVE: ***Ash, Morridge Moor, Staffordshire, January 2006***
An isolated ash tree and a lone figure, both awaiting dawn on a frozen outcrop in the North Staffordshire moorlands.

ABOVE RIGHT: ***Winking Man, Ramshaw Rocks, near Upper Hulme, Staffordshire, April 2007***
This anthropomorphic outcrop looks east to greet the sunrise over Morridge Moor with an impassive expression. Jutting out from Ramshaw Rocks, 'he' is seen to 'wink' when approached by road from Leek.

RIGHT: ***Ramshaw Rocks, sculpted, near Upper Hulme, Staffordshire, December 2006***
Bands of weakness in the Roaches Grit have been exploited by the actions of ice, water and wind to leave weird and wonderful shapes behind. No human hand has helped carve this elaborate form.

Hen Cloud, near Upper Hulme, Staffordshire, January 2006

Hen Cloud's unmistakable escarpment juts out from the plateau like a fin, between the hamlet of Upper Hulme and the start of The Roaches. 'Cloud' derives from the Old English word 'clud' meaning hill or rock.

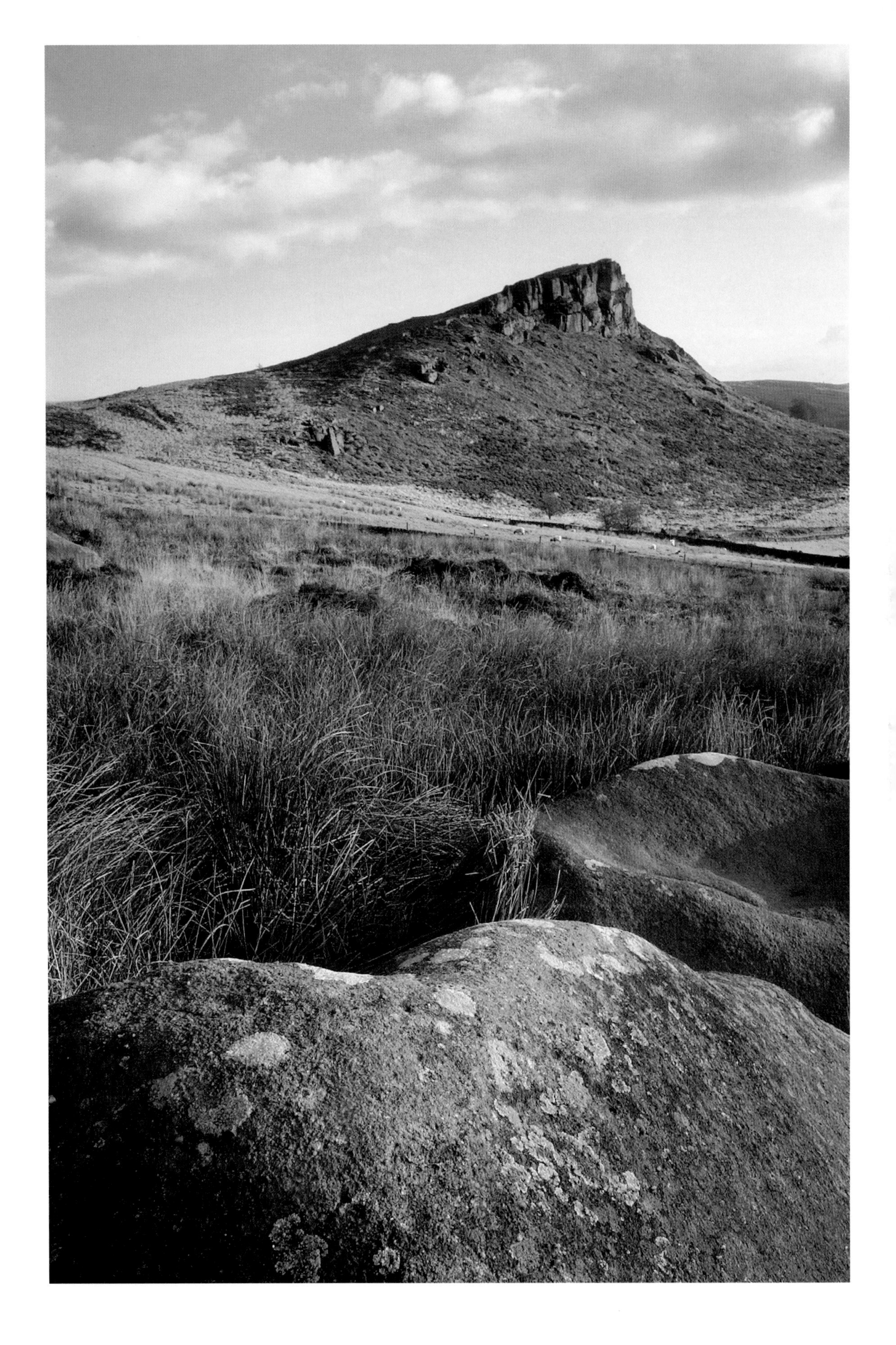

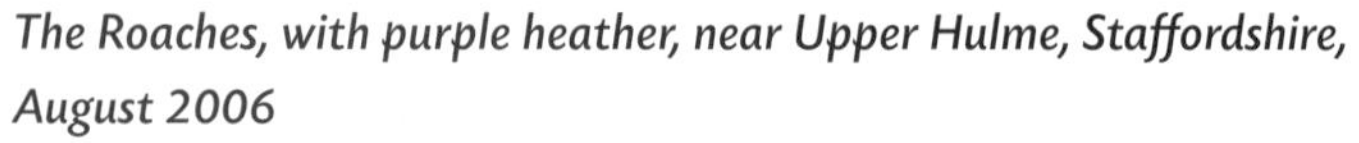

The Roaches, with purple heather, near Upper Hulme, Staffordshire, August 2006

Boulders of pink Roaches Grit are dwarfed by the vertical rock face of The Roaches rising above the bracken-carpeted moorland to a height of nearly 520 m. The name derives from the French 'les roches' meaning 'the rocks'. Once part of the Swythamley Estate, The Roaches were bought by the Peak Park in 1980.

Gateposts, The Roaches, near Upper Hulme, Staffordshire, January 2006

Oddly pink, foggy conditions created an unusual effect just after sunrise. Lining the gateposts up with the just visible sun enhances the relationship between the foreground and the unusual void where the horizon should be.

Larch woodland, The Roaches, near Upper Hulme, Staffordshire, February 2006

Larches growing at the base of The Roaches take on otherworldly properties when freezing fog curling among the fallen boulders and tree-trunks, accentuates the woodland's enchanted atmosphere. A rich green patina of lichen covers every surface.

LEFT: ***Doxey Pool, top of The Roaches, Staffordshire, September 2006***
In an exposed site on a small plateau topping The Roaches, a shallow pool nestles in eroded Roaches Grit. Due to both the effects of natural weathering and also the thousands of walkers passing this way each year, the rock has been broken down into particles of sand.

BELOW: ***Bosley Cloud, from below Roach End, The Roaches, Staffordshire, November 2006***
From the northern end of The Roaches escarpment, looking out of the Peak Park towards Cheshire, Bosley Cloud rises from the plateau between Bosley and Cloud Side.

RIGHT: ***Gib Torr, Morridge Top, Staffordshire, December 2004***
In the overcast light of a murky moorland morning, a burst of weak sunshine briefly transforms the subtle tones of over-wintering grasses, providing contrast with the solid outcrop of Gib Torr. It acts like a signpost to the larger and better-known formations of Ramshaw Rocks and The Roaches, a short distance to the south west.

LEFT: ***Old oak, Reapsmoor, Staffordshire, December 2005***
An old, and nearly hollow oak, clings onto life on wind-scoured farmland.

BELOW: ***Source of the River Manifold, Axe Edge, Staffordshire, April 2006***
The distinctive shape of Axe Edge dominates the skyline of the South West Peak, consisting of a cap of Roaches Grit reaching 551 m above sea level. Just above the source of the River Manifold, a few of the buildings of Flash can be seen. The village, at 463 m, is the highest in England.

RIGHT: ***Snowy fields, between Longnor and Sheen, Staffordshire, February 2004***
An inviting entrance to a snowy field in the farmland of North Staffordshire.

TOP: ***Dove Head and Upper Dove Valley, Derbyshire/Staffordshire, May 2006***
On an early summer morning Dove Head catches the first rays of sunshine while the surrounding valley remains in shadow. From Axe Edge this broad view takes in the farmland that gives rise to the River Dove and looks far beyond into the hazy distance. The rolling landscape is interrupted by the jagged outlines of Chrome Hill, Parkhouse Hill and High Wheeldon.

ABOVE: ***Axe Edge Moor, near Buxton, Derbyshire, April 2005***
Straddling parts of Cheshire, Derbyshire and Staffordshire, this is a sparse landscape of bog vegetation and deep channels, known as groughs, cut into the peat. Few rocks protrude from the thick peat layer. The moor, at 551 m, gives rise to the rivers Dove, Manifold, Dane, Wye and Goyt.

ABOVE: ***Cheeks Hill and Orchard Common, near Knotbury, Cheshire, April 2005***
This part of north east Cheshire's uplands adjoins the high moorland of Axe Edge. The blanket bog clings to the undulating sandstone bedrock, supporting low-growing vegetation and a few trees.

ABOVE: ***Three Shire Heads and Panniers Pool, Cheshire, Derbyshire and Staffordshire borders, April 2007***
Panniers pool on the right is fed by a spring and waterfall that empties into the River Dane. On the left the river flows under a packhorse bridge, marking the point where the three counties meet. Centuries ago this area was a lawless zone that fell between jurisdictions.

LEFT: ***Derelict field barn and Shutlingsloe, Wood's Moss, Cheshire, March 2006***
A slight snowfall cloaks the moorland of Wood's Moss. The setting sun flushes the terrain with magenta hues. The derelict field barn leads the eye to distant Shutlingsloe just breaking the near horizon's line.

RIGHT: ***Shutlingsloe, near Wildboarclough, Cheshire, December 2004***
The peak of Shutlingsloe is a distinctive high point at 506 m on Cheshire's eastern uplands. Its unmistakable profile can also be seen from Derbyshire and Staffordshire, with particularly stunning views from Axe Edge Moor. On this morning a temperature inversion caused low cloud to remain trapped in the valley, making Shutlingsloe appear as an island in a sea.

LEFT: ***Conifers and broadleaf woodland, Macclesfield Forest, Cheshire, May 2007***
Although primarily composed of conifers managed for logging, Macclesfield Forest includes a significant quantity of mature broadleaf woodland. Ferns and bluebells thrive in land set aside as a nature reserve.

ABOVE: ***Trentabank Reservoir, Macclesfield Forest, Cheshire, May 2007***
The heronry on the margins of this reservoir is home to around twenty breeding pairs, alongside the many species of waterfowl. The surrounding plantations have healthy bird populations, including crossbills, siskins and goldcrests living in the treetops.

Goyt's Moss, sunset over Cheshire, June 2005
This high moorland at the edge of Cheshire overlooks the plain on which most of the county sits. Goyt's Moss gives the impression of being on top of the world. Looking into the sunset a few fields can be seen in front of Manchester's urban sprawl in the far distance.

LEFT: ***Common Cotton Grass, Goyt's Moss, Cheshire, July 2004***
One of two members of the sedge family of plants, the other being Hare's Tail Cotton Grass, that transform the boggy uplands with carpets of fluffy white flowers in the summer months.

BELOW: ***A537 from Shining Tor, Goyt's Moss, Cheshire, April 2007***
Sandstone blocks protrude below the summit of Shining Tor, the Cheshire upland's uppermost peak at 559 m; the second highest, Shutlingsloe, rises in the distance. The panorama overlooks the transition from rough moorland vegetation to improved pasture, through which the Buxton to Macclesfield A537 road snakes.

RIGHT: Windgather Rocks, above Goyt Valley, Cheshire, May 2007

As the name suggests, this is a breezy location, the top of the edge being an exposed moor only partially covered by the conifers of Goyt Forest. The sandstone escarpment is popular with novice rock climbers as the ascent is short and fairly easy.

RIGHT: ***Dovedale in flood, near Ilam, Derbyshire, May 2006***
Spring in Dovedale is an event. Seasonal rains bring a surge of water down the limestone ravine, flooding sections of the River Dove. This shows one of the many weirs that dot the river, created to extend feeding areas for trout, resulting in better fishing.

Thorpe Cloud, Thorpe, Derbyshire, May 2006
Thorpe Cloud, alongside Bunster Hill, marks the entrance to Dove Dale. This limestone reef, seen from the wet meadow featuring Marsh Marigolds next to the River Dove, has a completely flat top, which is a significant landmark.

BELOW: ***Ilam Hall from St Bertram's Bridge, Staffordshire, May 2006***
Set in landscaped grounds bordered to the south and west by the River Manifold, Ilam Hall is a popular place to visit. On a stormy spring day after heavy seasonal rainfall the river is in full flood, taking on the brownish hue of peat and silt washed from upriver.

OPPOSITE:

ABOVE: ***Reynard's Cave, near Ilam, Dovedale, Derbyshire, May 2007***

Far above the River Dove's current course, evidence of water and boulder erosion is seen in the numerous caves that dot the valley's slopes. At Reynard's Cave, hidden from view by dense vegetation, an impressive natural arch signals the entrance to the hillside.

BELOW LEFT: ***Rushley Bridge, River Manifold, Staffordshire, March 2006***

A frozen Manifold stopped in its tracks underneath Rushley Bridge, not far from its confluence with the River Dove.

BELOW RIGHT: ***Upper Taylor's Wood, Dovedale, near Milldale, Derbyshire, May 2007***

Ash is an integral part of the calcareous woodland in Dovedale, helping to stabilise the rocky slopes. Considered to be some of the finest ash woods in the country, only a few pockets of ancient woodland exist here united by much secondary tree growth.

THIS PAGE:

Grindon Moor Barrow, near Grindon, Staffordshire, December 2005

The prominent round barrow occupies a lofty moorland position above the river valleys of the Manifold and Hamps. Just off Parson's Lane, north west of Grindon village, this barrow is easily spotted as it has a sycamore rooted deep into the mound itself.

Thor's Cave sunburst, near Wetton, Staffordshire, May 2007

Positioned in a crag 80 m above the River Manifold, Thor's Cave has a west-facing aperture through which afternoon sunshine pours, illuminating its interior where artefacts dating back 10,000 years have been found, making it one of the earliest recorded sites of human activity in the Peak Park.

TOP: ***Field enclosures, Wetton, Staffordshire, May 2006***
A patchwork of limestone walls, as far as the eye can see, define the green fields of a gently undulating landscape.

LEFT: ***Wolfescote Dale, Dove Valley, near Hulme End, Staffordshire, April 2006***
Standing tall above the valley floor, scarred and grooved limestone cliffs carved out by water erosion over millennia, form a distinctive part of the River Dove's journey.

ABOVE: ***Sheep in fields, near Wolfescote Hill, Hartington, Derbyshire, April 2006***
Friendly inhabitants of Dove Valley grazing fields, high above Hartington village, enjoy the spring sunshine.

Staden Barn, off Reynard's Lane, near Hartington, Derbyshire, April 2006
Two barns sit high above Hartington, the perfect place from which to survey the expanse of the Upper Dove Valley. The barns are elegant and well-preserved structures, built with great craftsmanship from locally quarried limestone, and are still in use today.

Sunlit beeches, Beresford Dale, Derbyshire/Staffordshire, October 2006

A gleam of sunshine breaks though the beech trees' canopy, accentuating the variety of colour shown in autumnal woodland. These trees stand at a bend in the River Dove in sheltered Beresford Dale.

Mixed hedging on limestone plateau, near Newhaven, Derbyshire, December 2005

The graceful silhouette of trees delineating a field boundary in an exposed location on a seemingly endless limestone plateau mostly cleared of trees.

***Above:* Nine Stones Close, Harthill Moor, near Birchover, Derbyshire, February 2005**
The circle's four remaining stones belie what was once a much larger monument, estimated to have been 14 m wide. Ranging from over 1 m to about 2 m high, they are the tallest stones in Derbyshire. The stones are also known as the Grey Ladies, owing to the legend that they are really women in petrified form, who dance at midnight. This moor is rich in other Bronze and Iron Age remains; and in the distance the crag of Robin Hood's Stride can be seen.

***Left:* Bluebell and oak, Harthill Moor, Derbyshire, April 2007**
Three forms of bluebell grow wild in Britain. The common (English) variety is the archetypal bluebell, easily identified by its nodding flowers that grow on one side of the stem. Also found is the invasive, non-indigenous Spanish Bluebell, resulting in a hybrid form which threatens to wipe out the native species.

ABOVE: ***Robin Hood's Stride, Harthill Moor, near Birchover, Derbyshire, July 2007***

This outcrop occupies a prominent position on Harthill Moor and has a unique profile. Interesting shapes are seen in the heavily eroded sandstone, the upper reaches exhibiting deep vertical grooves carved by flowing water. The name derives from a legend that Robin Hood strode from one tower to the other.

RIGHT: ***Spring Wood bluebells, near Alport, Derbyshire, April 2007***

Britain has 50 per cent of the world's population of common bluebells, which inhabit old woodland and are a familiar sight in spring. As they take a minimum of five years to develop from seed to bulb and longer still to establish a woodland colony, they are a protected species.

LEFT: ***The Cork Stone, Stanton Moor, near Stanton-in-Peak, Derbyshire, January 2006***
This sandstone outcrop, covered in centuries of graffiti, has weathered to an intriguing shape. Iron bars and carved footholds, added to make it easier to climb, are thought to date from the nineteenth century.

LEFT BELOW: ***Birch bracket fungus, Stanton Moor, Derbyshire, October 2004***
This kind of fungus is found on dead and dying birch trees, it is a common sight in autumn and plays a vital role in the woodland's lifecycle.

RIGHT: ***The King Stone, Stanton Moor, near Stanton-in-Peak, Derbyshire, November 2006***
An outlying marker of the Nine Ladies stone circle, the King Stone stands on the south west approach to the site. He is the now petrified fiddler to whom the Nine Ladies were said to have danced.

ABOVE: ***Arbor Low, near Monyash, Derbyshire, May 2005***
Viewed from the henge that encloses the space, the circle closely resembles a clock face raised up on an earth platform. Unpredictable stormy light transforms the scene: vivid green and bright white limestone contrasting with the shadowy plateau to the north.

RIGHT: ***The Nine Ladies, Stanton Moor, near Stanton-in-Peak, Derbyshire, November 2006***
Morning sunlight plays across the Nine Ladies stone circle and sets the birch woodland's autumn colours aglow. The legend of the Nine Ladies states that they were women caught dancing on the Sabbath and turned to stone for their sins. The surrounding landscape has many Bronze Age burial cairns among other ancient structures.

LEFT: ***Calcareous grassland, Lathkill Dale, Derbyshire, May 2007***
This NNR is idyllic, supporting a rich variety of limestone dale and river habitats. Early purple orchids and lady's bedstraw carpet the calcareous grassland in spring with magenta and yellow hues, later making way for pockets of the nationally rare purple Jacob's ladder in summer.

RIGHT ABOVE: ***River Lathkill, next to Bateman's House, Lathkill Dale, Derbyshire, May 2007***
The small river is crystal clear and supports a highly visible population of dippers and secretive water voles. Fringed by Wych Elm, ash and a diverse range of woodland plants, the river in the lower section of the dale is exceptionally shallow because of leakage into underground lead mines.

RIGHT BELOW: ***Pilsbury Castle, Pilsbury, Derbyshire, April 2007***
This limestone knoll was once the site of a small fort, of which only the motte (central earth mound) and deep boundary ditches are still visible. Situated above a historical crossing point on the River Dove, it is thought that the Normans built the 'castle' in the eleventh century.

Sudden sun towards Crowdecote, High Wheeldon, Staffordshire, June 2004

The limestone reef of High Wheeldon rises from the River Dove valley, acting as an impressive backdrop for the comparatively tiny field barn. The river, just out of sight behind a tree-lined bank, is little more than a stream gently meandering along the valley floor.

Parkhouse Hill, Dowel Dale, near Earl Sterndale, Derbyshire, April 2006

This spring, rising near Dowall Hall, is a tributary of the River Dove. In full flow after heavy seasonal rains, it meanders around the base of Parkhouse Hill, through calcareous grassland, home to many sheep and countless wildflowers.

TOP: ***Chrome and Parkhouse Hills, Staffordshire, June 2006***
The massive limestone reef of Chrome Hill emerging from the valley floor dwarfs the isolated hamlet of Hollinsclough. The hill is also known locally as Dragon's Back, a reflection of the fluted profile of its upper reaches. At the right is the pyramidal form of Parkhouse Hill, a much smaller but equally impressive reef.

ABOVE: ***Oak atop barrow on Harley Hill, Earl Sterndale, Derbyshire, January 2006***
The site of this round barrow, marked by a large oak, provides views of the Upper Dove Valley. The jagged crest of Parkhouse Hill sits below the horizon on the left, and Chrome Hill's serrated form is at the right.

Street House Farm, beech tree stand, Pomeroy, Derbyshire, January 2006

Typical of limestone pasture, mostly cleared of trees, are small pockets of woodland bordered by low drystone walls. Here is an example of a circular enclosure containing mature beech.

Heathfield Nook, near Buxton, Derbyshire, December 2005

A stand of beech just inside the south west border of the Peak Park. On this day, the coldest I remember at −14°C, it was difficult to stay in the woods long enough to take the photograph.

LEFT: ***Five Wells chambered tomb, Taddington Moor, Derbyshire, December 2005***
A snow-dusted view of the lofty Five Wells Tomb, a sadly ruined Neolithic monument. From the eastern end the tomb looks impressive, belying the damaged western end which collapsed after the supporting earthen mound was removed a couple of centuries ago.

LEFT BELOW: ***Cow Parsley and oats, Little Longstone, Derbyshire, May 2007***
White-flowered cow parsley, a common sight in hedgerows and meadows, grows at the fringe of an oat field. The scene glows with the first light of day, a hint of mist still lingering in the valleys beyond.

BELOW: ***Monsal Dale from Monsal Head, Derbyshire, May 2007***
The viaduct that once carried the Midland Railway, and is now part of the Monsal Trail, dominates the view towards Upperdale and Cressbrook. Here the River Wye carves a right-angled course through the limestone bedrock, creating a distinctive horseshoe-shaped valley.

LEFT: ***Weir on the River Wye, Monsal Dale, Derbyshire, May 2007***
Water thunders over this large weir with immense force, making a considerable impact in the tranquil tree-lined ravine.

ABOVE: ***Rubicon Wall, Water-cum-Jolly Dale, Cressbrook, Derbyshire, May 2007***
Rubicon Wall's bright limestone face is a striking backdrop for the millpond sited at a bend of the River Wye. The dam and weir were created to power the cotton industry at the adjacent Cressbrook Mill that closed in 1971.

RIGHT: ***Early purple orchid, Cressbrook Dale, Cressbrook, Derbyshire, May 2007***
Cressbrook Dale NNR is famous for its showy early purple orchids that cling to its grassy slopes from late spring.

LEFT: ***Peter's Stone and hawthorn, Cressbrook Dale, Derbyshire, May 2007***
Evening sunshine illuminates the dramatic, displaced limestone mass of Peter's Stone, standing sentinel-like at the dale's northern end. The unsettled geological structure is evident in the bare boulder scree.

ABOVE: ***Misty fields, Foolow, Derbyshire, December 2006***
Foolow is a typical limestone area with many drystone walls and some hedging enclosing the strip fields around the village. About 3 km to the north east looms Eyam Moor where the rock abruptly changes to sandstone.

RIGHT: ***Bettfield Farm, near Chapel-en-le-Frith, Derbyshire, July 2004***
A small farm sits at the top of the river valley where the seasonal tributary runs dry in the summer heat. When active, it feeds Black Brook that runs through Chapel Milton village where it joins the River Goyt.

ABOVE: ***Cave Dale, Castleton, Derbyshire, December 2007***
A steep-sided dry river valley containing a slight trickle of water in wet weather. Peveril Castle is balanced precariously on exposed limestone crags near the mouth of the dale. Thick morning mist pushes up from the valley floor and partially obscures the view of Win Hill behind.

RIGHT: ***Peveril Castle and Mam Tor, Castleton, Derbyshire, December 2006***
Perched on a ridge high above Cave Dale, with Mam Tor as a backdrop, this castle is an unforgettable sight. Today, only the square keep and some bailey walls remain to illustrate the former extent of the fortification. Founded after the Norman Conquest of 1066 by William Peveril, it was foremost in the defence of the Royal Peak Forest.

Castleton village in mist, Derbyshire, December 2006

From a vantage point above Cave Dale, Castleton is seen against a backdrop of Lose Hill and a distant Win Hill. Nestling in the valley floor, the village lies amid a network of enclosed fields, dividing the pasture into a typical patchwork pattern. On this cold December morning a fine layer of mist shrouded the base of the hills.

LEFT: ***Speedwell Cavern, Castleton, March 2007***
A typical chamber in the upper reaches of the cavern. All parts of this cave system have been thoroughly explored for lead, though it was only after the expense and hard labour that went into the construction of the 900 m long Grand Canal passageway, that it was discovered there were few productive galena deposits.

ABOVE: ***Winnats Pass, Castleton, Derbyshire, December 2006***
Contrary to a long-held belief that it was caused by a cave roof collapse, geologists now know Winnats was a tidal canyon on the sea floor around 300 million years ago. Subsequently buried by mud, it is only in geologically recent times that erosion has exposed the steep-sided, mile-long gorge with its irregular limestone pinnacles poking through the grassy slopes of its upper reaches.

RIGHT: ***Miner's snot, Blue John Cavern, Castleton, Derbyshire, March 2007***
Strange-looking deposits of calcite (calcium carbonate) and other cave minerals sometimes referred to as 'miner's snot' – for obvious reasons – are properly known as flowstones. They often take the form of overhanging curtains of rock and are a common sight in limestone caves.

LEFT: ***Chatsworth House, Chatsworth Estate, Derbyshire, October 2004***
Patchy afternoon sunlight illuminates this imposing stately home against a backdrop of autumn colour at Stand Wood. In the foreground, ridge and furrow patterns provide evidence of medieval farming practised in the area.

BELOW, LEFT: ***Birch trees in mist, Eaglestone Flat, near Curbar, Derbyshire, December 2006***
The Downy Birch tree is a variety suited to upland life as it thrives in poor soils. It is a tree typical of woodlands growing on sandstone moorland.

BELOW, CENTRE: ***Big Moor, Barbrook II stone circle and cairn, Derbyshire, November 2006***
This moorland site above Baslow is home to many examples of ancient relics. Barbrook II, the most visually impressive of these remains, is a complex structure consisting of a low drystone wall, including several standing stones, surrounding a central cairn. Shown here in the first light of dawn, it has an atmosphere of quiet dignity.

BELOW, RIGHT: ***Baslow Edge, above Curbar, Derbyshire, December 2006***
From the lichen-encrusted sandstone boulders of Baslow Edge, mist is seen lapping at neighbouring Curbar Edge's lower slopes. This phenomenon can be viewed from many high vantage points in the Peak Park throughout winter and early spring.

RIGHT: ***Curbar Edge after sunrise, Curbar, Derbyshire, November 2005***
The low-angle of early morning light reveals the grooved texture of Chatsworth Grit forming Curbar Edge. In the middle-distance, Baslow Edge interrupts the view south down the mist-filled valley. It is an excellent location for surveying the Chatsworth Estate and beyond.

River Derwent, Froggatt Bridge, Froggatt, Derbyshire, April 2007
The broad River Derwent flows under the village's seventeenth-century bridge. Cottage gardens slope to the water's edge and marginal meadow plants line the banks.

ABOVE: ***Froggatt Edge, above Froggatt, Derbyshire, February 2007***
Looking north west from Froggatt Edge, above the Derwent Valley, the distant shapes of Win Hill and Bamford Edge can just about be seen. Froggatt Edge is part of a distinctive sequence of sandstone escarpments, starting with Stanage Edge in the north and ending with Birchen Edge to the south east.

RIGHT: ***Stone circle, Froggatt Edge, above Froggatt, Derbyshire, December 2006***
This Bronze Age monument, also known as Stoke Flat circle, consists of eleven stones and is roughly 16 m wide. Although very close to the main path along Froggatt Edge, the site is so overgrown by bracken that it is easy to miss.

White Edge Moor, above Froggatt, Derbyshire, September 2006
The Longshaw Estate is transformed by intense golden light escaping from under a thick layer of cloud minutes before sunset. Rolling mist separates the trees of Sheffield Plantation and Granby Woods from the slopes of Eyam Moor rising behind.

LEFT: ***Sheffield Plantation, below White Edge Moor, Derbyshire, September 2006***
This shot, from the vantage point of White Edge Moor, shows the extraordinary spectacle of the mist curling up from the valley floor vividly backlit by the setting sun.

ABOVE: ***Fiery silver birch, Bolehill Quarry, Longshaw Estate, Derbyshire, November 2005***
Old millstones quarries invaded by silver birches provide a wonderful sight in the golden light of a late autumn afternoon.

ABOVE: ***Padley Gorge, Burbage Brook, Longshaw Estate, Derbyshire, November 2006***
The water of Burbage Brook carves its way through this wooded gorge as it tumbles down from Burbage Moor. In autumn, when most leaves have fallen, enough sunshine penetrates the canopy to form shifting pools of light, illuminating the russet hues of oak and beech.

LEFT: ***Millstone and beech, Yarncliffe Wood, Upper Padley, Derbyshire, November 2006***
Above Burbage Brook is Yarncliffe Wood, better known as Padley Gorge. Home to oak, beech, birch and alder, in autumn it becomes a riot of rich gold and red tones. An abandoned millstone sits in a pool of light, fringed by a carpet of leaf litter.

ABOVE: ***Millstone Edge, Surprise View, Derbyshire/South Yorkshire, November 2004***
A Chatsworth Grit outcrop on top of the edge marks the spot from which to appreciate the vista, colloquially referred to as Surprise View, which includes a large part of the Hope Valley's upper reaches. The village of Hathersage sits in the valley bottom directly below the edge.

RIGHT: ***The Mother Cap, Millstone Edge, Hathersage Moor, Derbyshire, January 2007***
At 8 m tall and worn into a characteristic pointed cap-shape, the Mother Cap forms an instantly recognisable feature on the plateau at the top of Millstone Edge.

ABOVE: ***Millstone Edge, looking towards Higger Tor, Derbyshire/South Yorkshire, November 2004***
Stratification in the rocks of Millstone Edge is typical of Chatsworth Grit. Many large outcrops dot the plateau's surface at the top of the edge. From here, they lead the way north east to flat-topped Higger Tor on the horizon.

ABOVE RIGHT: ***Burbage Brook, Hathersage Moor, Derbyshire/South Yorkshire, October 2006***
Burbage Brook rises on Burbage Moor near Stanage Edge on the Peak Park's north east margin. The brook winds past the remains of the hill fort of Carl Wark, which can be seen in the distance, on to Padley Gorge and beyond. Dippers and grey wagtails visit the dark, peat-stained waters.

RIGHT, ABOVE: ***Carl Wark, Hathersage Moor, South Yorkshire, February 2007***
On this natural, steep-sided plateau, the remains of Carl Wark hill fort can be seen, with Higger Tor rising in the distance. Constructed from sandstone boulders and earthen ramparts, it is possible that this one-acre site predates all the other Iron Age fortifications.

RIGHT, BELOW: ***Higger Tor, Hathersage Moor, South Yorkshire, March 2005***
This outcrop of Chatsworth Grit on the western edge of Higger Tor provides a distinctive foreground to the view of the Upper Derwent Valley beyond at a murky winter sunset. With twilight gathering fast it was a good time to practice some low-light photography, and these naturally sculpted boulders made an interesting silhouette against the fading sky.

Higger Tor, view to Millstone Edge, South Yorkshire, December 2006
Sometimes in the Dark Peak one is lucky enough to be above cloud level. Standing on the southern end of Higger Tor outcrop, watching the early morning mist consume the land was a magical sight. Out of the cloud rises Millstone Edge; below is the escarpment topped by Carl Wark hill fort.

Blacka Plantation, Blacka Moor, Sheffield, South Yorkshire, March 2006
Freezing fog hangs suspended in the pines of Blacka Plantation. Next to the A625 Sheffield to Hathersage road, this small woodland includes heath and wetland meadow on its margins. It is a newly established nature reserve and SSSI.

Silver birch against the sunset, Burbage Moor, South Yorkshire, January 2007
The same lonely birch tree, now denuded of leaves, somehow made all the more isolated by a deadening layer of snow.

Silver birch, Burbage Moor, South Yorkshire, August 2006
In August the high moorland is vivid with swathes of purple heather. This solitary birch is the only vertical interrupting a characteristically horizontal landscape. Just inside the boundary of the Peak Park, Burbage Moor separates the outer limits of Sheffield from open countryside.

LEFT: ***Ringinglow sunrise, Sheffield, South Yorkshire, January 2007***
Below Ringinglow village there is a clear view across the Limb Brook Valley to the high ground of north east Derbyshire. Although part of the Ecclesall Ward of Sheffield, the village retains a sense of rural independence from the city, situated as it is at the very edge of the Peak Park.

BELOW: ***Redmires Reservoirs, Hallam Moors, Sheffield, South Yorkshire, October 2006***
These three reservoirs are just inside the Peak Park, occupying a location between the populated area of Lodge Moor and the moors leading west to Stanage Edge, via Stanedge Pole. The distance from the centre of Sheffield is less than 10 km.

Stanage Edge, view towards Hathersage, Derbyshire, August 2005
Looking south towards Hathersage and the valleys beyond. The afternoon light on Stanage Edge warms the magenta heather, prominent among the rocks and repeated on the moors in the middle distance.

ABOVE LEFT: ***Stanage Edge at sunset, above Hathersage, Derbyshire, October 2006***
Stanage is a magnet for climbers who love the challenge of the Chatsworth Grit's structure. Looking north from the eastern end of the escarpment reveals the extent of the 6.5 km long cliff-face, making it the most unforgettable of the Peak Park's sandstone edges.

ABOVE: ***Grouse pool no. 6, Stanage Edge, Derbyshire, August 2005***
One of the many early twentieth-century basins to be found on top of the edge, designed to collect rainwater for grouse to drink.

LEFT: ***Stanage Edge in snow, above Hathersage, Derbyshire, January 2007***
Looking beyond the road down to the village of Hathersage, the last of the afternoon sunshine illuminates these snow-capped boulders on top of the escarpments eastern end. Its name is a corruption of 'Stone Edge', and the Chatsworth Grit was quarried for millstones, many of which can be found abandoned on its slopes.

LEFT: ***Overstones Farm, North Lees Estate, Derbyshire, April 2007***
Surrounded by bracken-covered moorland on all sides, this lonely farmstead nestles below Stanage Edge just off the Hathersage Road.

ABOVE: ***Mam Tor, Back Tor and Lose Hill, from Winatts Head, Derbyshire, December 2006***
Known locally as the Shivering Mountain, Mam Tor is composed of unstable sandstone/shale strata prone to slippage after heavy rainfall and frosts. The remains of the A625 Stockport to Sheffield road are seen on the north east side of the ridge. It has not been rebuilt since the 1974 landslide. Mam Tor, believed to mean 'Mother Hill' perhaps because of its breast-like shape, is the site of an Iron Age fort. Further along the ridge a second landslip at Back Tor leads up to Lose Hill.

RIGHT: ***Lose Hill and Back Tor, near Castleton, Derbyshire, December 2006***
Patchy sunlight catches the ridge of Lose Hill and the bump of Back Tor landslip, highlighting Only Grange Farm on the valley floor. This view from the side of mighty Mam Tor shows the hill and tor framed against the shadowy backdrop of Kinder Scout.

Cairn and footprints, Kinder Scout, Derbyshire, January 2007
This stone cairn is just above William Clough on the Hayfield approach to Kinder Scout. As this cairn is unmarked on the map it will, for the time being, remain of unknown origin and purpose.

The Vale of Edale, Derbyshire, April 2007

What is commonly termed Edale is a collection of hamlets, established in the thirteenth century as cattle farms along the River Noe, known as Upper Booth, Barber Booth, Grindsbrook Booth – where the Pennine Way begins – Ollerbrook Booth and Nether Booth. Overlooked by the Kinder Plateau to the north, Grindslow Knoll appears as a recognisable bump on the horizon catching the warm morning light.

Kinder Scout, looking towards Kinder Reservoir and Hayfield, Derbyshire, January 2007

Standing a little below the 624 m triangulation point on the slopes of Kinder Scout's upper eastern edge, the undulations and outcrops present in the combination of Kinderscout Grit and blanket bog are revealed. Covered in deep drifts the terrain appears untouched by human influence, but the snow hides extensive peat erosion caused by many footprints.

At the top of William Clough, Kinder Scout, Derbyshire, January 2007
A prominent yet nameless landmass at the top of William Clough. I rested at this spot, experiencing a feeling close to complete isolation in the uninterrupted snow and silence, save the whistling wind and the occasional call of a red grouse. In the last light of day, exhausted and with very cold feet, I picked a path through the drift and back down to the world below.

***ABOVE, LEFT:* Kinder Downfall, Derbyshire, January 2007**

The River Kinder starts life on the Kinder Scout plateau then drops off the edge of the steep escarpment to become the longest waterfall in the Peak Park at 30 m. In deep winter, the normally surging Kinder Downfall sometimes freezes. Conversely in summer it can be almost completely dry.

***ABOVE:* Win Hill and Ladybower Reservoir, Hope Valley, Derbyshire, November 2006**

Win Hill, at 462 m, composed of Kinderscout Grit, towers over the larger of the two parts of Ladybower Reservoir. Its forested slopes, planted with conifers, are picked out against the fading twilight.

***LEFT:* Win Hill, Hope Valley, Derbyshire, August 2005**

Seen from halfway up the side of Bamford Edge, Win Hill is framed against a backdrop of the Kinder Scout Plateau with which it is connected via a ridge. Seen clearly in silhouette the conspicuous bump, known locally as 'The Pimple', gives the hill its characteristic shape.

Bamford Edge, view to Ladybower Reservoir and Win Hill, Derbyshire, December 2006
A broad vista unfolds from the top of Great Tor on the fractured Kinderscout Grit of Bamford Edge, looking across to the cone-shaped Win Hill and beyond to Ladybower Reservoir. The natural drama is heightened by stormy weather, transforming the heather and bracken with sudden golden light.

LEFT: ***Seven Stones of Hordron at sunrise, Hordron Edge, Derbyshire, December 2006***
This 16 m wide circle of ten stones, is a less well-known monument than others in the Peak Park. Occupying an elevated moorland position, it has views of Stanage Edge, Bamford Moor, Win Hill, Lose Hill, Derwent Moor and far away Kinder Scout. It is well worth a visit, if you can find it among overgrown sedges and bracken.

BELOW LEFT: ***Whinstone Lee Tor, Derwent Moor, Upper Derwent Valley, Derbyshire, November 2006***
From this tor of jagged sandstone there is an impressive view of Ladybower Reservoir far below. At 410 m up it is possible to get an idea of the scale of the Upper Derwent Valley. Beyond Ladybower lies the Kinder plateau, Bleaklow Hill, Alport and Howden Moors.

BELOW CENTRE: ***The Salt Cellar at sunset, Derwent Edge, Upper Derwent Valley, Derbyshire, August 2007.***
Derwent Moor is home to many weathered Kinderscout Grit outcrops, the shapeliest being the Salt Cellar, which can be recognized from the valley floor far below. The last rays of sunshine cast a warm glow, providing soft side lighting that reveals the formation's contours rising above a carpet of purple heather.

BELOW RIGHT: ***Derwent Reservoir towers, Upper Derwent Valley, Derbyshire, November 2005***
These impressive towers on the dam wall dividing Derwent and Ladybower Reservoirs are seen here shortly before the annual floodwater flows over the tops of this dam and that of Howden Reservoir above.

LEFT: ***Ladybower Reservoir mirror panorama, Upper Derwent Valley, Derbyshire, November 2005***
Ashopton Bridge divides Ladybower Reservoir: this is the smaller of the two sections adjoining the Derwent Reservoir. The photograph was taken early in the morning, before a breeze could disrupt the perfect reflection on the water. The hill behind is a mix of broadleaf woodland and enclosed farmland extending up the escarpment of Derwent Edge above.

BELOW LEFT: ***Ladybower Reservoir reflections, Upper Derwent Valley, Derbyshire, November 2005***
On a perfectly still early morning reflections in this huge reservoir have a symmetrical beauty. The mixed broadleaf woodland looks glorious in late autumn, particularly with a frosting of ice crystals.

BELOW: ***Grouse butt, Birchinlee Pasture, Upper Derwent Valley, Derbyshire, November 2006***
One of the numerous grouse butts, or shooting covers, to be found on this moorland. This high point looks across to Howden and Derwent Moors and a small part of Howden Reservoir can be seen below.

Alport Castles and The Tower, Alport Dale, Upper Derwent Valley, Derbyshire, November 2006
The Tower stands as a crumbling pinnacle separated from the adjacent rocks of Alport Castles, an SSSI. This landslip is a fine example of the unstable shale strata that creates dramatic features such as this and Mam and Back Tors to the south.

Cranberry Ness, Howden Moor, Upper Derwent Valley, South Yorkshire, February 2007
Cranberry Ness stream trickles down a deep peaty clough (ravine) in the blanket bog-covered Howden Moor before it empties into the young River Derwent flowing from the moorland plateau's upper reaches.

The Kissing Stones, Bleaklow, Derbyshire, January 2007
An intimate portrait of the Kissing Stones, lying scattered among the sandstone boulders of the Wain Rocks on Bleaklow. After a long hike up a gradual incline starting at the Snake Pass road from Sheffield to Glossop, the sight of these distinctive rocks is a reassuring sight. They are one of the few landmarks within the Peak Park's largest wilderness.

FURTHER READING

Geology

Broadhurst, Fred, *Rocky Rambles in the Peak District* (Sigma Leisure, 2001).

Cope, F. Wolverson, *Geology Explained in the Peak District* (Scarthin Books, 1998).

Archaeology

Barnatt, John, and Smith, Ken, *The Peak District: Landscapes Through Time* (Windgather Press, 2004)

Edmonds, Mark, and Seabourne, Tim, *Prehistory in the Peak* (NPI Media Group, 2001).

Marsden, Barry M., *Burial Mounds of Derbyshire* (privately published, revised edition 1994).

Woodland

Blight, Graham (ed.) *Exploring Woodland: The Peak District and Central England* (Frances Lincoln, 2006)

Conservation and ecology

PDNPA:	www.peakdistrict.gov.uk
	www.peakdistrict-nationalpark.info
Natural England:	www.naturalengland.org.uk
The National Trust:	www.nationaltrust.org.uk

Department for Environment Food and Rural Affairs (DEFRA):
www.defra.gov.uk

Acknowledgments

My deepest thanks go to the following people who helped make this book possible:

Dr Fred Broadhurst for patiently advising me about the geology of the Peak District and for answering all my questions. Sarah Viner at the University of Sheffield Archaeology Dept., for reading my notes and for her invaluable comments. Mirren Halsall for her fair and thorough editing skills. Craig Dewberry, for his patience and support.

Other thanks go to everyone who over the years has encouraged me to pursue my creative dreams.

Prints from the book are available from
www.fran-halsall.co.uk

ABOUT THE PHOTOGRAPHY

Digital editing

It is my job as a landscape photographer to record faithfully the natural world as it is with as little modification as possible. This is I why I spend a vast amount of time waiting for the right lighting conditions to suit the subject. I do not rely on digital post-processing to recreate something that was not right in the first place; therefore it is vital to get the exposure correct in camera so that digital adjustments are kept to a minimum, preserving the image's integrity.

I use Adobe Photoshop for all digital editing work, using adjustment layers to enhance photographs selectively. To establish the correct range of contrast I use Levels, and to control the colour of a photograph (if it needs it) I use Colour Balance – that is my standard workflow. Occasionally I use Hue/Saturation either to reduce or increase the intensity of a colour that I feel has not recorded faithfully at the time of capture.

Exposure composite

Because the camera is not as sophisticated as human vision it causes problems when recording contrast, which is the extremes of tonal range – black at one end and white at the other. A common situation being that if shadows and midtones are correctly exposed, then the highlights will be 'burnt-out' or overexposed simply because the latitude (sensitivity of the recording medium i.e. film or digital CCD sensor) cannot cope with the range of contrast.

When shooting with film the way around this problem is to use a neutral density graduate, a filter which fades from darker to clear glass, by putting the darker part of the filter over the brighter part of the image, thereby balancing the exposure difference. While this is an excellent method, it does lead to occasional problems such as having the graduation line in the wrong place because it does not line up with the scene in front of the camera.

Working digitally allows for another possibility and this is the technique I have come to favour. By taking two images that are in essence exactly the same except that one frame is exposed for the majority of the scene, and the other is underexposed for the problem highlight area, then these two images can then be blended in the computer to create one perfect exposure. This method eliminates the problem caused by having a graduation line in the wrong place, because the fade between the two images can be tailored to suit the subject. However if anything moves between the frames, then the two exposures will not line up so this method is not always appropriate.

Panoramic stitching

As I was developing my visual style I began to feel somewhat restricted by the standard proportions of my camera. I wanted to expand, to go beyond the confines set by the 3:2 ratio of the CCD sensor. The natural step was to start taking multiple photographs in sequence and to combine them into panoramic images. This allows me to make images that are as long as necessary in order to suit the subject – I could potentially record an entire 360-degree. This technique lends itself particularly well to photographs of wide-open spaces taken from elevated viewpoints, and to moorlands and mountainous scenes.

On average, it is a case of overlapping and blending three separate photographs, providing an expansive enough view especially if taken with a wide-angle lens. The more complex the subject, the greater the number of photographs necessary to make the final panoramic image. Considering that the photographs used to make a panorama may already have been subject to an exposure composite, the creation of a panoramic image is the lengthiest and most complex process that I undertake.

TECHNICAL NOTES

Page	Description	Focal length	Aperture	Shutter speed	Polariser filter
half-title	Granby Wood	20mm	f/22	various: 0.5–1 sec	yes
title	Stanage Edge	20mm	f/22	1 sec	yes
4–5	Upper Derwent Valley	78mm	f/32	various: 5–10 secs	no
9	Kinder Scout	17mm	f/11	0.4 secs	yes
10	Bleaklow Head	24mm	f/22	1/8 sec	yes
12l	Tissington Spires	17mm	f/22	1/20 sec	yes
12r	Blue John Cavern	17mm	f/22	121 secs	no
13	Bolehill Quarry	131mm	f/11	1.3 secs	no
14	The Wheel Stones	17mm	f/22	0.4 secs	yes
16	Morridge Moor	23mm	f/22	1/5 sec	yes
18	Bleaklow	17mm	f/22	0.6 secs	yes
19	Common spotted orchid	73mm	f/5.6	1/125	no
20	Hay meadow	19mm	f/16	1/60 sec	yes
22	Backlit common oak	17mm	f/22	various: 1/8 & 0.6 secs	yes
23l	Meadow Place Wood	17mm	f/14	various: 1/20 & 0.3 secs	yes
23r	Pines	20mm	f/22	various: 0.4 & 0.5 secs	yes
24	River Wye	21mm	f/14	0.4 secs	yes
26	Reflected clouds	17mm	f/22	various: 0.3 & 0.5 secs	yes
27	Dafar Bridge	20mm	f/22	0.3 secs	yes
28	Gib Hill barrow	17mm	f/22	various: 0.5 & 0.8 secs	yes
29	Arbor Low	17mm	f/22	various: 1/6–1 sec	yes
30	Petroglyph	36mm	f/22	1/5 sec	yes
31	Morridge Top Farm	17mm	f/16	1/160	yes
32	Field enclosures	75mm	f/32	5 secs	yes
33	Ruined field barn	12mm	data not recorded		no
34–5	Blake Mere	17mm	f/22	various: 1/5–1.3 secs	yes
36–7	Morridge Moor	40mm	f/22	25 secs	no
38al	Ash	17mm	f/22	6 secs	no
38ar	Winking Man	31mm	f/7.1	1/60 sec	yes
38b	Ramshaw Rocks	17mm	f/22	various: 1/4–1.6 secs	yes
39	Hen Cloud, boulder Detail	21mm	f/22	1/8 sec	yes
40	The Roaches	19mm	f/16	1/25 sec	yes
40–1	Larch woodland	20mm	f/22	13 secs	no
41	Gateposts	17mm	f/22	1/6 sec	no
42a	Doxey Pool	19mm	f/22	1/4 sec	yes
42b	Bosley Cloud	24mm	f/22	various: 0.5–1.3 secs	yes
43	Gib Torr	17mm	f/22	various: 1/15–1 sec	yes
44	Old Oak	17mm	f/22	5 secs	yes
44–5	Axe Edge	17mm	f/22	various 1/15–1/10 sec	yes
45	Snowy fields	data not recorded			
46–7	Dove Head and Upper Dove Valley	98mm	f/32	0.5 secs	yes
46	Axe Edge Moor	17mm	f/22	various: 1/10–0.3 secs	yes
47	Cheeks Hill and Orchard Common	17mm	f/22	various: 0. 3–1 sec	yes
48a	Three Shires Head and Panniers Pool	17mm	f/22	various 1/6 & 1/5 sec	yes
48b	Derelict field barn and Shutlingsloe	17mm	f/22	various: 1/20 & 0.4 secs	yes
49	Shuttlingsloe	100mm	f/32	1/6 sec	no
50	Conifers and broadleaf woodland	17mm	f/22	5 secs	yes
51	Trentabank Reservoir	17mm	f/22	various 1/6–1.3 secs	yes
52–3	Goyt's Moss	40mm	f/22	3 secs	yes
54	Common cotton grass	100mm	f/3.5	1/350 sec	no
54–5	A537 from Shining Tor	17mm	f/22	various: 0.4–2.5 secs	yes
55	Windgather Rocks	17mm	f/22	various: 1/5–0.8 secs	yes
56l	Thorpe Cloud	17mm	f/22	various 1/13 & 1/10 sec	yes
56r	Ilam Hall from St Bertrams Bridge	17mm	f/22	1/10 sec	yes
57	Dovedale in flood	17mm	f/22	1/13 sec	yes
58a	Reynard's Cave	17mm	f/16	1/6 sec	yes
58bl	Rushley Bridge	20mm	f/22	0.3 secs	yes
58br	Upper Taylor's Wood	17mm	f/16	1/13 sec	yes
59	Grindon Moor Barrow	24mm	f/22	0.3 secs	yes
60	Thor's Cave sunburst	17mm	f/22	various: 0.4–1 sec	no
61a	Field enclosures	24mm	f/22	various: 1/8 & 1/5 sec	yes
61bl	Wolfescote Dale	30mm	f/22	1/15 sec	yes
61br	Sheep in fields	17mm	f/13	1/40 sec	yes
62–3	Staden Barn	17mm	f/22	both: 1/25 sec	yes
64	Sunlit beeches	19mm	f/22	0.4 secs	yes
65	Mixed hedging on limestone plateau	22mm	f/8	30 secs	no
66a	Nine Stones Close	17mm	f/22	0.5 secs	yes
66b	Bluebell and oak	17mm	f/14	1/80 sec	no
67a	Robin Hood's Stride	24mm	f/16	1/80 sec	yes
67b	Spring Wood bluebells	17mm	f/14	1/80 sec	no
68a	The Cork Stone	17mm	f/22	various: 0.8 & 1.6 secs	yes
68b	Birch bracket fungus	100m	f/6.7	1/8 sec	no
69	The King Stone	17mm	f/22	0.4 secs	yes
70–1	Arbor Low	21mm	f/22	0.4 secs	yes
71	The Nine Ladies	17mm	f/22	various: 0.4 & 0.8 secs	yes

Page	Description	Focal length	Aperture	Shutter speed	Polariser filter
72	Calcareous grassland	17mm	f/14	various: 1/250 & 1/125 sec	yes
73a	River Lathkill	17mm	f/14	1/5 sec	yes
73b	Pilsbury Castle	17mm	f/22	1/20 sec	yes
74	Sudden sun towards Crowdecote	40mm	data not recorded		no
75	Parkhouse Hill	17mm	f/22	1/10 sec	yes
76a	Chrome and Parkhouse Hills	22mm	f/22	various: 1/5 & 1/4 sec	yes
76b	Oak atop barrow on Harley Hill	17mm	f/22	various: 8 & 10 secs	no
77a	Street House Farm	40mm	f/22	4 secs	yes
77b	Heathfield Nook	24mm	f/22	0.5 secs	no
78–9	Five Wells chambered tomb	17mm	f/22	various: 1/8–1/5 sec	yes
78	Cow parsley and oats	17mm	f/16	various: 1/4 & 0.4 secs	yes
79	Monsal Dale from Monsal Head	29mm	f/22	1/4 sec	yes
80	Weir on the River Wye	19mm	f/22	various: 1/8–0.3 secs	yes
81a	Rubicon Wall	17mm	f/16	various: 1/125 & 1/30 sec	yes
81b	Early purple orchid	184mm	f/4	1/200	no
82	Peter's Stone	27mm	f/22	1/8 sec	yes
82–3	Misty fields	163mm	f/32	1/10 sec	yes
83	Bettfield Farm	38mm	f/27	1/6 sec	no
84	Cave Dale	29mm	f/22	various: 0.8 & 5 secs	yes
85	Peveril Castle and Mam Tor	70mm	f/32	1 sec	yes
86–7	Castleton village in mist	40mm	f/22	1/4 sec	yes
88	Speedwell Cavern	17mm	f/22	90 secs	no
88–9	Winatt's Pass	34mm	f/22	0.3 secs	yes
89	Miner's snot	70mm	f/22	8 secs	no
90a	Chatsworth House	85mm	f/27	1/8 sec	no
90b	Birch trees in mist	17mm	f/11	1/80 sec	yes
90–1	Big Moor	17mm	f/22	various: 0.6–2 secs	yes
91a	Curbar Edge after sunrise	17mm	f/22	0.4 secs	yes
91b	Baslow Edge	22mm	f/22	1/8 sec	yes
92	River Derwent	29mm	f/22	1/6 sec	yes
92–3	Froggatt Edge	17mm	f/22	various: 0.6–3.2 secs	yes
93	Stone circle	17mm	f/22	various: 0.5 & 1.6 secs	yes
94–5	White Edge Moor	21mm	f/22	various: 1/6–3.2 secs	yes
96l	Sheffield Plantation	200mm	f/32	1/6 sec	no
96r	Fiery silver birch	17mm	f/22	0.4 sec	yes
97a	Padley Gorge	17mm	f/22	various: 1.3–10 secs	yes
97b	Yarncliffe Wood	20mm	f/22	2.5 secs	yes
98–9	Millstone Edge	17mm	f/22	various: 1/6–1/4 sec	yes
99	The Mother Cap	17mm	f/13	1/25 sec	yes
100l	Millstone Edge	17mm	f/22	1/8 sec	yes
100r	Burbage Brook	19mm	f/22	various: 1/8–1/6 sec	yes
101a	Carl Wark	17mm	f/22	various: 0.4 & 0.5 secs	yes
101b	Higger Tor	17mm	f/22	various: 0.5–4 secs	yes
102–3	Higger Tor	17mm	f/22	various: 1/8–0.8 secs	yes
103	Blacka Plantation	17mm	f/22	4 secs	no
104–5a	Silver birch	23mm	f/22	1/6 sec	yes
104–5b	Silver birch against the sunset	84mm	f/18	30 secs	no
106	Ringinglow sunrise	163mm	f/32	various: 1/13–1/5 sec	no
106–7	Redmires Reservoir	21mm	f/22	various: 1/13–1/10 sec	yes
107	Stanage Edge	17mm	f/22	various: 0.3 & 0.5 secs	yes
108–9a	Stanage Edge at sunset	21mm	f/22	various: 0.8 & 2 secs	yes
108–9b	Stanage Edge in snow	19mm	f/22	various: 1–2 secs	yes
109	Grouse pool no.6	23mm	f/8	0.3 secs	yes
110–11	Overstones Farm	163mm	f/22	1/10 sec	yes
110	Mam Tor	39mm	f/22	1/4 sec	yes
111	Lose Hill and Back Tor	75mm	f/22	various: 1/10–0.6 secs	yes
112–13	The Vale of Edale	70mm	f/32	various: 2–3.2 secs	yes
112	Cairn and footprints	17mm	f/22	1/4 sec	yes
113	Kinder Scout	17mm	f/22	1/30 sec	yes
114–15	At the top of William Clough	17mm	f/22	various: 1/13–0.4 secs	yes
116	Kinder Downfall	36mm	f/22	1/10 sec	yes
116–17a	Win Hill and Ladybower Reservoir	32mm	f/22	various: 15–55 secs	yes
116–17b	Win Hill	70mm	f/22	various: 1/10–1/6 sec	yes
118–19	Bamford Edge	17mm	f/22	1 sec	yes
120a	Seven Stones of Hodron at sunrise	17mm	f/22	various: 1/8–1.3 secs	yes
120bl	Whinstone Lee Tor	20mm	f/22	1/4 sec	yes
120–1	The Salt Cellar	17mm	f/16	various: 1/20–1/4 secs	yes
121	Derwent Reservoir towers	17mm	f/22	various: 1/10–0.4 secs	yes
122–3	Ladybower Mirror mirror panorama	22mm	f/22	various: 1/4–0.3 secs	yes
122	Ladybower Reservoir reflections	70mm	f/25	0.8 secs	yes
123	Grouse butt	28mm	f/22	various: 1/10 & 1/8 sec	yes
124l	Alport Castles and The Tower	22mm	f/22	1/5 sec	yes
124r	Cranberry Ness	17mm	f/22	0.4 secs	yes
125	The Kissing Stones	32mm	f/22	0.8 secs	yes